CW01067112

Last of the
Raj Memsahibs
1929 to 1945

Memoirs of a Cavalry Officer's wife

Lorraine Gradidge

With a Foreword by Sir Mark Tully K.B.E.

First Published 2013 by

Podkin Press
Podkin Wood,
High Halden,
Kent TN26 3HS

ISBN: 978-0-9559483-1-2

Contents

Acknowledgements

My mother wrote this book in the late 1970's. I promised her that I would do my utmost to get it published. It has taken longer than I wanted but at last this has been achieved.

Francis Gradidge.

My many thanks go to:-

My Mother for writing her story.

Sir Mark Tully for reading her story and writing the foreword.

Sue Marina Farrington for reading her story and correcting the mistakes.

Sir Michael Parker for continually badgering me to do something about it.

John Mulligan and the Podkin Press for all the work in producing it.

Joanne Farrant for all her work in designing the book.

General Mike Swindels and Prue Swindels for their help and encouragement.

Foreword

By Mark Tully

Lorraine Gradidge, the widow of a British officer who served in an elite cavalry regiment of the Indian army during the last years of the Raj, wrote her memoir to counter the customary portrayal of the memsahibs. She wanted to provide "an 'authentic account" of her life as a military memsahib. Which was certainly not the life of idle luxury surrounded by servants treated like slaves so often portrayed. In that way her memoir is an important contribution to history. It's also a fascinating autobiography of a woman of great courage who had to face danger and disease, endure loneliness and suffer from nostalgia for her homeland, live with the uncertainty of long separations, and bear with the life of an army officer's wife, a life that often irked her. She lived by the rules of that life, supporting her husband and making an invaluable contribution to the success of his career, so with justice she says in her preface, "I feel that the wives of those men who lived in a sense with their husbands permanently on active service deserve a little of their husbands' reflected glory".

Lorraine Gradidge's husband was an officer in Guides cavalry a unique regiment permanently posted on the remote, unsettled, and dangerous North West Frontier of the Indian Empire. The officers were permanently on standby to repel raiders from ferocious tribes across the frontier and put down insurrections. The tribesmen shot with deadly accuracy, so a regimental wife had to live with the fear that her husband would not return from one of these encounters. When not actively engaged an officer's life centred on polo and the camaraderie of the mess. It was a life wives were largely excluded from, hence the loneliness and at times boredom that Lorraine Gradidge describes.

Officers' wives also had to face the dangers of everyday life in India during the thirties and forties, particularly the health hazards. Lorraine Gradidge nearly lost a daughter to dyptheria and her own life during an extremely difficult child-birth in an army hospital where there was no privacy. A complicated hierarchy of servants was considered essential for maintaining the style expected of an officer in the Guides. Servants needed delicate handling by memsahibs. Lorraine Gradidge was justifiably proud that not one of her servants left her during the four years her husband was away on active service during World War 2. That of course was only one of the separations she had to suffer. During the long wartime separations affairs developed endangering marriages. Lorraine Gradidge avoided that hazard. She did have an admirer but that was a platonic affair.

Much of the narrative of this memoir is set in the dying days of the Raj. It seems incredible that such a life still existed right up to the Second War. There were endless balls in Calcutta when the Gradidges visited the city for polo tournaments. Governors were treated like Royalty and the Viceroy was royalty. Ostentatiously arrayed Maharajas, although they had surrendered much of their power, still demanded to be regarded as royal not just by their subjects but by the British too. Among the British snobbery was rampant, and protocol strictly observed. Along side this splendour there was the squalor of India, the squalor created by the all-prevailing poverty. India was at that time one of the poorest nations of the world. The sub-heading of one of the chapters in this memoir is "The splendour and the squalor."

Lorraine Gradidge also describes her life as a child in Calcutta during World War One. Her father was Head Partner of the leading firm of solicitors. Not much seems to have changed between then and the second world war when I spent my early childhood in Calcutta, except that the triumph of the motorcar had begun and the only horse-drawn vehicles I can remember were cabs we knew as tikka-garis. The horses were usually on their last legs and the cabs on their last wheels. We too had a European nanny, a lady who I came to be very fond of although she could be very strict, especially when enforcing bans on playing with Indian children and learning what she called scornfully "the servants language." In Lorraine Gradidge's time snobbery had created such a strict class-system within the British community that children with European nannies were not allowed to play with children whose parents could only afford Indian nannies. I don't remember a ban like that when I was young, but I do know that anyone involved in retail was considered at the bottom of the social hierarchy in the Calcutta business community of which my father was a member.

Lorraine Gradidge tells her story with unwavering honesty. She admits to boredom, loneliness, and longing for her homeland, and yet when she came to leave India for the last time she wrote of "leaving behind so much she had loved". When she parted with her two faithful servants all she could do was hold their hands while all three wept. India had woven its spell. She had played a role in the partnership which governed the Indian Empire. The tiny number of British civil servants and army officers who served the Raj could never have held India together if they had not had Indian partners. The Indian army was the most remarkable partnership, founded on the mutual respect of British officers and Indian men. After World War One, Indians were also commissioned in some regiments. To play their role in this partnership British officers' wives had to command respect. They would not have done so had the image of them as vacuous, mindless women, which Lorraine Gradidge complained about, been accurate. She is surely justified in claiming not only a little of the glory of her husband but also the glory of the army he served in. It is all too often forgotten that the Indian Army of the Raj expanded during World War One to provide more than one million soldiers to fight on the side of the allies. That number more than doubled during World War 2 in which Lorraine Gradidge's husband fought.

Preface

As I write this in Lymington in 1978, the widow of an Indian Cavalry Officer I am a member of a dying breed. The last of the English "Memsahibs" left India over thirty years ago, at the time of partition, where a large number of them had spent the best years of their lives, between the ages of twenty and forty.

So much has been written of us in a derogatory way that the general picture of an English woman in India is a mindless female, with loose morals, whose sole interest in life was drinking cocktails, having dances and parties, and ordering Indian servants about like slaves. I feel therefore, that before my allotted span is up, I should give an authentic account of the life of just one of the vast number of English service wives, who "followed the drum" with their husbands, in that vast complex and sometimes daunting continent of India between the two wars and during the last.

My husband belonged to a famous Indian Cavalry Regiment "Queen Victoria's Own Corps of Guides", sometimes irreverently called "Gods Own" by fellow officers in other Cavalry Regiments!

This Corps was unique, in the Army, consisting as it did, of one Cavalry Regiment with mounted band, and one Infantry Battalion. All wearing the same uniform and Regimental badges, sharing the same Mess and Chapel, and permanently on the North West Frontier of India in the same station named Mardan, except in the two world wars, when both units served overseas, on active service.

They were raised in 1846, by Sir Harry Lumsden as a Corps of Frontier Guards. The officers were the British and their illustrious names made their Regiment famous. Sons followed Fathers -

some, such as the Battyes for four generations; and many were the officers in the 1930's, when I arrived, whose Fathers were well known Generals, famous and decorated men.

This is no place to write of the many deeds of heroism of those Guides of the past, both British and Indian, whose names have gone down in history and this book is not meant as such. Their deeds have already been written of by Younghusband of the Guides, and many others, and also in the two volumes of the Regimental History. Mine is only a very personal story, but I feel that the wives of these men who lived in a sense with their husbands permanently on active service, deserve a little of their husbands reflected glory.

Map of India 1929-1945

Introduction

Childhood in India 1914 to 1918

Throughout these memoirs I refer to India as a whole Continent, as all its contents occurred before the Partition of India into the separate countries of Pakistan and India.

At the beginning of the first World War, my Father returned to his firm of lawyers in Calcutta, Orr Dignam & Co. as Head Partner, taking my mother, younger brother and me with him. He had had polio from birth, so was always very lame and would have been rejected from any of the Services, apart from that he was now over forty.

My years of childhood in India are full of the happiest memories. My mother was not only elegant and charming, but was one of those rare human beings who emanate joy and happiness to all around her. Her sympathy and sense of humour made all troubles taken to her into little ones. Any pain shared with her seemed to fade and become non-existent, and any joke shared with here became hilarious.

She was, in my opinion, the life-line to her husband, as well as her children. Our English Nanny, known as Nana (Of solid Yorkshire stock), has also left a strong impression in my life, imperturbable, she epitomized the Nannies of those days, in her stiff Eton collar and hard cuffs, on her blue print dress with starched apron in the mornings, and her soft grey dress and crisp collar and cuffs, which she wore to take us out in the afternoons. I can see her so vividly getting ready for our afternoon drive, rolling the front of her hair, into a false 'sausage' across the top of her forehead, then tying the ends of her starched white bow under her chin, and pinned on the top of her head. On this she placed her dark blue straw and velvet bonnet, finishing the job by stabbing two long hatpins through it from side to side. It was a never ending source of wonder to me how she could bear the pain of the pins through her head, where I always thought they went, and she let me think so. She told me that each line on her forehead counted as a hundred years, so I always thought that Nana was five hundred years old.

Each day after our rest, in the large tent like mosquito net which fell from ceiling to floor, including our three beds and large main ceiling fan, we drove to the Eden Gardens in Calcutta. Here we met to play with the other white children with their English Nannies. Woe betide the white children whose parents could only afford an Indian Ayah, or almost worse, an Eurasian Nanny. The upper class English Nannies would not dream of allowing us to mix with them, be they the sons of Generals or Judges.

When darkness began to fall, we drove home in state in our Victoria carriage, the Nannies own mode of transport. The liveried coachman and groom mounted the driving box, having lit the oil lamps on either side. I remember how carefully he managed to make one match light both, by cupping the match in his hands to run round the carriage, and a happy and weary little boy and girl climbed in each side of their indomitable Nana with her kind face and large bust, and set off for home at a quiet and steady clip-clop, with monkeys jumping and gibbering in the trees we passed.

As the shades of evening fell, the gas lights along the roads were lit, the shadow in the carriage of its occupants constantly reoccurred on one side and then the other, this fascinated me, as we steadily made for Alipore and its spacious comfortable houses, surrounded by large gardens in which the rich English men lived in those days.

Sunday was the climax of the week for me, and my brother, as on this one day our Father was not at his office, and so instead of the Eden gardens, we went to the Zoo, dressed in our best, and Nana in white pique. We played with the English children with their respective white Nannies, until at 5 p.m. when our Father arrived in his chauffeur driven car to pick us up and take us to that utterly wonderful invention, the Bioscope.

Nana was despatched home in state in her Victoria, while joy of joys, 'Boykins' and I sat enthralled each side of our Father watching yet another episode of the never ending adventures of 'Pearl White' (the current film star) whose hair raising escapes from death each week, kept us in eager suspense until the following Sunday.

These Calcutta winters sped happily by, with riding and tennis lessons on our two excellent grass courts, and then, as March approached, and the heat of the sun was deemed too great for European women and children, we set off for the Himalayas, complete with ponies, dogs and servants, accompanied by our beloved Mother. The train journey of forty eight hours to the foothills was a glorious adventure. The strange smells and sounds at each station, the water carriers call of "Tunda Panee Mussalman" or "Tunda Panee Hindu" (cold water) as he walked along the platform, a taut goat skin on his back, selling his refreshment to the third class passengers, into whose eagerly cupped hands and brass mugs he doled out a portion. There was also the cry of the pan and betel and wallah, ringing his bell, that was so exciting, to us children, in our first class carriage. We always had a tin bathtub filled with ice, surrounded by lemonade and soda water, on the floor of our compartment, as well as bottles of boiled water, (We never drank unboiled water or milk). Our servants travelled third class and would come along the platform at each halt to dust the carriage, and make up our beds for the night.

The arrival in the dark at Dehra Dun was tremendously exciting. A car drove us through the clear cold night to a Dak bungalow where we slept till morning. We then embarked in dandies (a canvas chair on poles, carried by six coolies, taking turns to carry the poles on their shoulders) for Mussoorie, the hill station four miles above us. These men were very strongly built hill men, cheerful laughing men, who rarely washed, and whose strong body odour I can remember to this day.

Life in a hill station where in those days, we spent six months of each year, was full of activities for children of which there were many. We had parties and picnics, surrounded by the majesty of range after range of Himalayan mountains and beyond the distant towering snow giants of the Himalayas with Nanda Devi outstanding at 25,645ft, lit each evening by seeming magic hues of rose and gold, in from the setting sun in the brief Indian twilight.

Crystal clear air and bright sun by day added to the joy of living and for us children nothing could have been happier. There was a dear little school, run by two stalwart English sisters, which we had to attend each morning. We each had our own ponies to ride, and a syce running beside us. I received my first information of the facts of life from my syce. When I asked him why my pony was getting so fat, he informed me, that she had a Bacha - baby - inside her. It puzzled me for years to know how a full grown foal had got inside her.

When the monsoon came and torrential rain flooded the country, my Mother would go back to Calcutta to join my Father, who had been working in the sweltering heat, and then they both came back for his leave. We then all returned together to our large comfortable house, with its smiling salaaming servants to greet us, marble floors to walk on and again cars to drive in.

That there was a bloody war being waged on the other side of the world was beyond our comprehension. It did not touch our young lives, but each night I used to pray for "Nana's nephew at sea". Being in the navy with a beard, I always saw his face on a Players cigarette packet.

At the end of the war and my Father's retirement, we said good-bye to our Indian home, and our kind and faithful servants, and returned to England and the miseries of English boarding schools. I remember getting out of the car and running back to kiss the old house, our happy home, goodbye, and being asked by Nana how I'd got all that red dust on my face!

Captain J H Gradidge (Reggie)

Chapter One

"What know they of England who only England know"

Arrival and First Impressions

My appearance on the shores of India at Bombay in 1929 at the age of nineteen, with a baby son of six weeks old, was hardly welcoming.

My husband, Reggie, was then a Captain rejoining his Regiment, after being Chief Instructor to the Iraq Army for two years, and had described Mardan to me in glowing terms. Here the Guides had built, and established a unique Mess, which housed a number of priceless antiques in stone and brass, and was surrounded by a park-like garden with immense trees and lawns, and filled with beds of roses and English flowers.

They had built their own beautiful Regimental Chapel, the only one in India, and also made the two best grass polo grounds in India.

Naturally after his descriptions of this Eldorado, so near the mountains of Chitraland Kashmir, I looked forward with the greatest excitement to my arrival. In those days it took us three weeks by sea to reach India from England, and the wrench of leaving my home, and Mother, to whom I was devoted, for at least three years, was a sad parting.

At Port Said "Coaling" took place, when gangs of chanting blackened coolies carrying sacks of coal on their backs, walked on planks from quay to steamer all night and day, covering us, the ship, and everything in it with coal dust.

As we approached the Port of Bombay, memories flooded back, and I felt thrilled at the prospect of getting to know this vast land, which I only vaguely remembered. The wild confusion on the docks in the humid heat was somewhat bewildering, but we had a reserved compartment on the "Frontier Mail", a train which would take us to Nowshera on the Frontier in forty eight hours.

This had all been arranged by a suave Parsee gentleman, in a tall shiny hat from Grindlay & Co. He met us with the Indian bearer he had already engaged for us, and assured us that everything was in order, and all we had to do was, give him our keys, meet him on the train later that night, and we should find our beds already made up in our compartment. So we abandoned our luggage to red garbed screaming porters, pointing vigorously at the brass number plates on their arms. The only pay they received was two annas (equivalent to 60p today) for a load, which they carried on their backs, so the more they could grab, the better.

We left this wild melee and took a taxi to the famous Taj Mahal Hotel, driven by an apparently mad Sikh, who blew his horn non-stop, and drove without pause, straight at any moving object, except of course a sacred cow. When I said "Do be careful you nearly killed that man" he replied "If you do not drive at him, how he get out of way?" The drive through squalid streets filled with humanity, in every stage of dirt and poverty, appalled me, as did the starved scavenging dogs, the vegetable matter spilled on the pavements, and the crawling deformed beggars among it all.

Arriving at the Hotel was like stepping into a different world. Cool marble floors, with swirling fans overhead, and silent bare-footed servants in immaculate white, offered such a contrast and relief.

It was while sipping our ice cold drinks on the palmed verandah that my husband was handed a telegram from his Colonel; which tersely read, "Do not bring Wife or Child with you. No accommodation". This greeting from my husband's beloved Regiment filled me with a foreboding that perhaps all was not going to be milk and honey. We sent a telegram to an Aunt of mine whose Army husband was stationed at Jallunder on our route north. "Leaving baby and Nanny with you tomorrow midnight", and prayed that they would be there to meet us. Bless them they were.

The journey North in an immensely long train, with two huge British built engines pulling it, and invariably driven by an Anglo-Indian driver in a dirty topee, and two Indian assistants, to coal it, was fascinating.

We flew past mud built villages in which the women pounded clothes in the extremely dirty village pond, often with a buffalo in it, almost submerged, with small naked boys perched on their backs, scrubbing them vigorously. The dust was appalling and got inside one's mouth, hair and clothing despite the choice of shutters, dark glass, or wire mesh on all the carriage windows.

The halts at wayside stations seething with squatting, sleeping, and cooking humanity, and the strange cries of the hawkers were full of interest, which countered the layers dust and the staggering heat of the sun.

The further north we journeyed, the better the physique of the population, and as we reached the Punjab, more and more fine looking men appeared. Tall and handsome, with acquiline features, and many with blue eyes and paler skins. Their rakish pugarees, and upturned twirled moustaches, gave them an air of superior grandeur, greatly added to by their embroidered waistcoats, voluminous trousers and a swaggering gait to which one felt they had a right.

The stops became fewer and farther between, as we sped North, and at each station hoards of Indians tried to board the train, and the hordes inside resolutely pushed them off. Some climbed on to the roof or hung on the outside until they dropped off exhausted at the next stop or climbed in the windows. At some of these halts we walked along to a restaurant car for a fairly indifferent meal, whilst our bearer tidied and dusted our large and comfortable compartment. Then, after miles of sun baked plains the air took on a freshness and chill, and beyond we saw distant blue mountains and now many of the men wore pathan poshteens which came originally from Razmaki Waziristan. These coats lined with goat's and sheep hair are an invaluable garment against an icy wind, but were generally exceedingly smelly, as the skins had not been properly cured.

To me the tribesmen of Northern India are the handsomest men in the world, and by now many were carrying rifles over their shoulders, or a knife in their belts. Soon after crossing the guarded Attock Bridge on the Frontier of India, we approached our destination Nowshera. Here we were met by a Major of the Guides Cavalry, who said, "Pity you brought your wife old boy, we've no bungalow for you. You can stay with us for a day or two but then you will have to pack her off to the hills!" We drove twenty miles through a cold clear night, the sky a vast panoply of sparkling stars, to our future home, Mardan, and were greeted by our hostess passing the Colonel's bungalow on our way waving and calling a greeting as we went by. This cheered me somewhat, and after a 'chota' peg of whisky, by a blazing log fire, I began to feel a little happier.

Reggie was elated to be back with his beloved Regiment, and take over command of "A" Squadron, but the question of where I, my baby and Nanny were to go, was not tackled until the next day. I had no intention of being 'packed off to the hills', until I had to. Our host eventually said "Well there is the polo bungalow, but God knows what state it is in, it hasn't been inhabited since the Missionaries left it after their little boy was murdered there over a year ago. We can get your kit sent over there. You both better go and have a look at it tomorrow".

I later learnt that these brave Danish Lutheran Medical Missionaries had remained on in the district, despite their tragedy, continuing to spread the Gospel, and help all who came to them. Ultimately they built a Christian Hospital near Mardan. This is indeed true faith.

Mercifully I did not set eyes on my new home for 24 hours. It turned out to be a dilapidated bungalow, on the far edge of the two polo grounds, and very near a most unsavory village called Rubbi, renowned for housing all the local bad lads. It's windows were broken, and the mud floor and walls spattered with the dung of the buffalos and goats who had made it their winter quarters. Standing in the middle of these large dung pats were all our cases from England. I sat on one of them and burst into tears but somehow we cleaned it up. There are many willing hands in an Indian Regiment, furniture was hired, wedding presents and china unpacked. We sent for our baby son and nanny and settled down for the five remaining weeks of the 'cold weather'. I was now able to inspect the 'Home of the Guides', Mardan, for myself.

It was an oasis of greenery, in a barren land, thanks to our forebears. The cantonment in which we lived, as all British residential areas were named, consisted of a cluster of large bungalows, surrounding the Mess, each with its very large grass garden, beautifully kept and full of sweet peas, which grew to an enormous height, roses and stocks and in fact most English flowers. Luckily the river of the mountains of Swat provided a plentiful water supply and the superb winter climate meant that English 'green fingers' had made a counterpart of Home throughout the years. Everyone in India referred to England as Home. Leave was always called Local Leave or Home leave.

The Bazaar and village were very near, but on the North West Frontier white women did not go far afield alone, and on long hacks we were accompanied always by husbands or Indian orderlies.

When I first arrived we had no electric light, so hurricane bhutties, kerosene oil lamps with handles for carrying, were used. In the hot weather a punkah was pulled to and fro by a 'punkah - wallah' sitting, or eventually lying, and pulling it back and forth with his big toe. This somewhat somnolent position often sent him to sleep, from which he was rudely awakened by an irate shout from the Sahib inside, and set going again. This was during the hot weather in the afternoon siesta only, when the officer had been up and out since 5 a.m., and would then take violent exercise on the polo grounds, schooling ponies, or playing polo, from 5 p.m. till 7 p.m.

In those days it was customary to wear what was known as a cholera belt, when lying naked under a punkah, or fan, to ward off tummy chills, dysentery or worse.

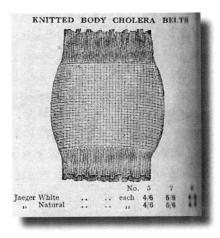

I got to know The Guides and their wives before alas having to leave my husband and set forth for the hills as they were always referred to, although the Himalayan mountains rose to heights of well over 25,000ft.

We went to Kashmir from Mardan, as it was our nearest hill station, although still two days drive away. It was a direct order from our Colonel that no women or children were allowed to remain in the plains after April 1st, so off we had to go.

Chapter Two

"Oh to be in England now that April's here"

Kashmir and Gilgit

We set off for Kashmir with our car piled high with luggage. and bedding rolls, known as holdalls, tied to the mudguards for our five hour drive heading north over the Murree Hills and down into the valley of the Jhelum River, over a rough, narrow and stony road, cut- into the mountain side, along the ravines, with the rushing river a sheer drop below us. This was cluttered with logs floating down to the plains and constantly kept on the move by men jumping on them precariously and parting them with long poles. We were frequently stopped by falling boulders, or minor landslides, and often had to wait for several hours for coolies to make a somewhat dangerous passage for the car to continue.

We had a to spend a night in a dak bungalow en route. These were primitive, but belong to some of the memories I cherish most.

After a long hard day, to relax in a hot tin bath-tub and then to lie back in long chairs outside on a perfect starlit night, with the roar of the tumbling water below and the Himalayan mountains towering above, had a kind of magic about it. Meanwhile, our Bearer had lit log fires in our bedrooms, and made our beds up on charpoys, (a wooden frame interwoven with webbing) which, though hard, were exceedingly comfortable.

As soon as the local Khansamah, or cook, saw our approach we heard the squawks of an unfortunate chicken whose throat was being cut and this was served as our dinner when we decided to have it. The invariable menu at a Dak bungalow was clear soup (surprisingly good), moorghi or very tough chicken, and caramel custard, pronounced 'caramelly custard'.

Unfortunately, at our start next morning, our elderly nanny, the self same starched nana of Calcutta days, fell down the steep stone steps with the baby in her arms and gashed her leg bare to the bone. Of course there was no doctor near enough to call and we thought she would bleed to death. Reggie drove madly back down the road for aid, leaving me to pad her leg with sheets and towels and pour brandy down her throat and eventually the baby's too.

After eight hours he returned with an Indian doctor who put her on the dining room table and sewed her leg with 40 stitches and told us to get her to Srinagar as fast as possible, before gangrene set in. So we laid her on the back seat, put the luggage on the roof and drove non-stop to the only English Nursing home there was. I and the baby, with a large bump on his head, went into a houseboat on one of the many lakes in Srinagar. My husband had to return to Mardan as his weeks leave was over.

Poor old Nana remained in the Nursing home for two months, nearly lost her leg and cost us a small fortune, which on a Captain's pay of only 900 rupees (£72) a month meant we were stony broke.

A houseboat is not to me, a very attractive or hygienic way of living, as the owner's boat is tied astern, where he and his numerous children live, and where all the cooking is done and all the refuse thrown into the river. After a month of this and as the temperature rose in Srinagar, we proceeded to move up to Gulmarg which stands in a beautiful valley 9,000ft above the sweltering plains below. We had an appalling trip on a local bus, which I and a pregnant wife from the Guides, shared. The Kashmiri driver stopped half way and demanded double the agreed price before he would continue. After a couple of hours of furious argument, with my baby screaming his head off, we paid up and advanced to Tanmarg, where we changed on to ponies for the final four miles up to the beautiful little valley of Gulmarg. The baby was carried by two men in a dandy on their shoulders and after much bargaining, coolies were engaged to carry our luggage on their backs.

This they held with a rope and browband across their foreheads. The Kashmiri hill men are of incredible strength and both tough and cheerful. One man was known to have carried a piano on his back up to Gulmarg. They were exceedingly poor and dirty and most of then had lice in their hair, but were always laughing and I liked them very much better than their brethren of the plain below who would cheat and swindle whenever possible.

Life in Gulmarg was a strange mixture of loneliness and gaiety. I could not say I was happy the first summer, of the eight I was eventually to spend there. My friend and I shared a wooden hut, buried in huge pine trees. All the Marg, or valley, was surrounded by these huts where women and families lived, but neither of us knew anyone then and our hut was isolated and in poor condition. I loathed the insects and beetles we shared it with, particularly the huge flying variety which banged into the lamps and into our face at nights. There were two excellent eighteen hole golf courses, and a small Club house, but apart from the Bazaar and Nedous Hotel, which consisted of individual huts up a steep incline to the main building, not much else.

The climate was superb, with air like champagne, and once the men came up from the plains there was a great deal of gaiety and fun. We could go off trekking to Lhasa or Gilgit. Reggie and I did, in fact, trek to Gilgit to stay with the Resident some years later, with a caravan of small ponies, known as tats, to carry our food and belongings. Sleeping in the Dak bungalows en route, or tents and eating all our meals on the way. At one of these picnics I suddenly noticed to my horror, that I was covered with fleas. I rushed behind a rock and tore off all my clothes which were literally crawling with these hopping little insects. I was told it was the flea season on that part of the route and we hurried on as fast as possible. We walked most of the way, only occasionally using our ponies. We were soaked to the skin with torrential rain a good deal of the time, but the towering Himalayan peaks, and the scenery around us made it all a memorable trip. We crossed 14,000ft passes, dropping into lovely small valleys between, and we often had to cross precarious rope bridges over rock strewn fast flowing rivers. When we arrived at Astor near Gilgit itself we met our hosts in their delightful home, it was fantastically beautiful. We were on the lower slopes of the famous Nanga Parbat mountain. In an unsuccessful attempt to climb it in 1932, six sherpa porters and four Germans, lost their lives having reached a height of 23,000ft. To look up to its snow covered summit almost floating 25,000ft above us on a moonlight night was a superb experience.

As Gilgit was the country in which polo originated, our host Sir George Gillam, suggested that my husband might like to take part in a game, which they still played in its highly original form. Reggie, a madly keen polo player with a handicap of six, was all for it, so we went to watch the proceedings. The local band turned out and squatted on the ground, making a ghastly din on drums and pipes. The players, there looked to be about 10 a side, assembled in the middle of the ground with my husband amongst them riding a pony so small that his feet nearly touched the ground, he was 6ft 3in. The ball was thrown in the air, and play commenced. This consisted of galloping madly up and down the ground wildly hitting in the direction of the ball, whether in the air, or on the ground. If a player was clever enough to catch it, he carried it through the goal posts (there were no boundary lines), midst wild shouts of "shabash", "well done" and a fanfare on pipes and drums. In the middle of all the scrimmage my husband stopped and dismounted leading his mount and peering about on the ground. No one paid the slightest attention to him dashing madly past and at him and I could not imagine what he was doing. There are no set chukkas in this game, which continues until animals and men are exhausted. Eventually he stooped and picked something from the ground. A loud cry of "Mila Ha", "Found" rose from the spectators and he continued to play to the end. When he rode over dripping with sweat, we asked him what he was looking for, "My teeth!" he replied. He had had two front teeth knocked out in a previous accident and wore two false ones. He had coughed while galloping, and saw them sail through the air between his ponies ears. He said, "I was damned if I was going to go all the way back to Kashmir without two front teeth!"

Returning to life in Gulmarg, with its golf and many glamorous evenings dancing at the famous Nedous ballroom. We dined in style in full evening dress, the men wore white ties and tails, and waltzed until the small hours. There were of course no roads or vehicles, so on these occasions one had to ride one's tat (pony), pinning our long full skirts round our waists, and cantering across the Marg in the dark, followed by our panting 'tat-wallah' (the owner) running behind. It sounds very hard on the pony owner who would squat outside until we returned to our beds. But they lit charcoal braziers, which they all sat round laughing and joking and we gave them baksheesh (extra tips) and cigarettes, which they shared and passed round in cupped hands, each man taking a puff or two, from the same cigarette and they all seemed happy, used as they were to the harshness of their mountain life.

Most of us hired one man and his pony for five months and paid him a generous daily wage throughout, whether one used his pony or not, and this, for him, was a good living wage. With this came a strict understanding that he never hired his pony to anyone else, otherwise the poor beast would be working twelve hours a day, as many did.

So passed my first taste of Indian Hill Station life. This meant four months separation and then two months leave for the husband to join his family, before we returned together for the winter, or cold weather as it was called, to the plains below. If the man was a keen fisherman, one could always descend to the plain of Srinagar, 3,000ft lower and go out camping to fish the many rivers for magnificent trout, or even Mahseer, on the wide Sind river. This too was a most delightful way of camping with plenty of servants to cook and make life comfortable, a shikaris, or ghillie to accompany one amidst the magnificent surroundings.

On our return to Mardan, we had to take on another bungalow allotted according to one's husband's rank, unpack all our belongings again and settle down for the next six months. Whilst we were away our husbands had moved into bachelor quarters consisting of a long bungalow with single rooms and had their meals in the Mess. This hot weather routine in his life consisted of rising before sunrise, for early dawn parade, after which he would return and to the mess swimming pool where his bearer would be waiting with his mufti or civilian, clothes. After a shave and shower he would plunge into the ice cold spring fed pool, before changing. This was no ordinary swimming pool, as it was like a room in the mess garden, enclosed in fine wire mesh, to keep out the flies, mosquitoes and even sand flies, with their menace of malaria, and sand fly fever.

Breakfast too was served in it, after which the officer would bicycle off to his office for his mornings paperwork. Lunch in the delightful mess under a cool punkah, or fan, and then to his room for a siesta. By 5 p.m. he would be in jodhpurs (pronounced to rhyme Spode not, as now always referred to in England as Jodpaws). It is an Indian word coming as it does from the state of Jodhpur worn as white trousers in Indian dress. He would now move up to the polo grounds for a couple of hours intensive schooling and training of his polo ponies, or play a game of what was known as station polo. (rather like a 'knock up' at tennis). Then it was back to his bachelor quarter for a bath and change into white mess kit for a formal dinner in the mess. In the hot weather, this would be on the lawn outside, with overhead lighting and fans and then a game of buck or bridge and a drink or two, before cycling back to his quarter for bed.

Chapter Three

"Ready aye Ready"

Life on the North West Frontier for a man, and a woman with.......

The Guides

The Cold weather in Mardan could be very cold indeed with snow on the surrounding hills. We had fires, and wore English winter clothes. The six months in these circumstances were delightful in many ways in a glorious climate, with sun all day, but I found myself in a strictly male world. For the men it was perfect. They had their Regiment, their Mess, which was sacrosanct, and no woman ever allowed inside it. All the married officers were obliged to dine there at least one night a week, in full Mess Dress, with the Band playing. Many a lonely night I spent listening to the Band in the distance, sitting by myself in my bungalow thinking of England.

On Mess Guest nights which were fairly frequent, when all the lovely mess sliver trophies shone in candlelight and the dinner was over, toasts to the King drunk, the port passed on a small silver trolley rolled round the mess table, and the ultimate departure from the dining room, the fun began. All the officers were young and many wild, and somewhat dangerous games took place. Such as climbing round the room, six to eight foot above the floor. Or one man blindfolded with a bludgeon of tightly rolled newspaper in his hand shouting "Are you there Moriarty?" and the chosen victim obliged to shout 'yes', dodging, or getting a tremendous clout on his head. 'Cockfights' and a rough house generally ensued, which became quite fierce. One distinguished officer had half his large moustache forcibly shaved off, the day before he headed the march of the Guides Infantry to active service further along the frontier. He was not pleased. Many Messes had ceiling cloths on top of which were rats and snakes in the beams and much fun was had by officers shooting their revolvers through the cloth to bag an active rat.

It was regarded as 'soft' to play tennis although we had three excellent grass courts. A Guide was supposed to play polo or school ponies, even if not for himself, for the Regimental polo team. Shooting game was permissible, or hockey with the men. Indians are exceptionally good hockey players but the tennis courts were very little used. Strange as in other parts of India, a lot of tennis was played.

It was indeed a man's world, a woman did not seem to belong to it. Army brothels had been banned in 1890 by the then reigning Vicereine, so all this physical exercise helped, I assume, to put sex out of their minds. A love affair with a brother officer's wife would certainly have meant immediate expulsion from the Regiment.

Our lives were lonely and at times dull, whereas our husbands lives were completely fulfilled with their horses, mess, polo and constant alert for the possibility of active service.

We were in a frontier station, where there were frequent raids on villages, from tribesmen across the border which we were protecting. Afridis, Wazirs, Mahsuds and all the Pathan outlaws, indulged in constant raids of pillage and rape, swooping down on the hapless villages within reach of the border and the role of the Guides was always to be prepared to repel, or out manoeuvre such attacks and pursue and re-attack these marauders. One squadron was always on twelve hours notice for active service. So there was anxiety, as well as loneliness, to contend with. No wonder, on guest nights, the men let themselves go, and became like small boys again. They always bicycled to the Mess and many a bachelor officer was found next morning, snoring his head off beside the path to his quarters, lying happily asleep in a nearby bush. His patient bearer would collect him and get him back, bathed, and dressed for parade that morning.

I had had a very happy life in England before I married with May Week Balls; skiing in Switzerland, dances, flirtations and pretty clothes, so that I was somewhat surprised to find myself among a group of young good looking men who appeared to think women didn't exist! This is one of the reasons I believe, that they and their Indian Soldiers got on so well together. The Indians themselves kept their women hidden away in Purdah, and in a strange way, I felt their British Officers were copying them. Not that I suggest we were not free to go about as we pleased, but I felt that there was no real place for me in this masculine world. Had I not been most deeply in love with my husband, I could not have endured it. It was a very insular life, as the Brigade we belonged to, was nine miles away at Risalpur. Here was stationed another Indian Cavalry Regiment, a British Cavalry Regiment and a Gunner Battery. Few of us had cars in these early days, so it was not easy to fraternize frequently with them.

We had to entertain ourselves with ourselves and at dinner parties I found the sole topic of conversation was polo and polo ponies. They would sit until the early hours after dinner, talking of nothing else, which I found exceedingly boring. When I arrived, there were in my husbands regiment, many Officers who were the sons and grandsons, of very famous forebears, who had made history in India with the famous Guides. It seemed to me that they had dedicated their lives to this regiment of a foreign land and almost erased the female sex from their thoughts. The rule was that no Officer might get married before he was thirty and, even then, he had to ask his Colonel's permission to get engaged, and to someone regarded as suitable. In some ways, I thought they were like a bunch of grown up public school boys turned into men and very brave and fine men they were. The top ten places at the passing out parade at Sandhurst, in those days, were allotted the opportunity of joining the Indian Army, so we obviously had in our Regiment, the pick of Officers, most of those who had the chance, chose the Indian Army, for the advantages of both sport and pay. They drew a higher pay than the British Army as their service was to be permanently abroad.

In those early thirties I happened to play tennis fairly well, having been coached at the Queen's Club in my teens, but I could find no one to play with except the Indian Marker (professional), and as I did not find sitting by the polo ground every day, gossiping and knitting, while our men folk galloped madly up and down the ground with four or five ponies each to exercise, and their attendant orderlies to sustain them with cool drinks and new polo sticks between chukkas, madly exciting, I took myself off to play tennis with the Marker.

The winter months on the Frontier had glorious weather and riding in the morning before breakfast was a joy. In the cool early mist which seems to lie all over Northern India at sunrise and the strange smells of villagers cooking on dried dung, the stillness and space was fascinating. The famous Peshawar Vale Hunt (P.V.H.) was not too far away for us to hunt with them on Sundays, mostly Jackal, but quite often we found a fox. One had to be up in the dark, as all scent had gone by 11 a.m. and the meet was at dawn.

The Master was an Officer from an Indian or British Cavalry Regiment and hounds were brought out in couples from many famous English packs. The going was over rough and treacherous country, with very large Irish banks and the pace was extremely hot. Hounds sometimes crossed the Frontier and on one occasion a friend riding side-saddle, had a very bad fall, breaking her pelvis. It was from a village over the border that four lusty tribesmen were called on for help and they carried her on a charpoy to the nearest motorable road and then returned to their life as outlaws.

After hounds went home, most of us repaired to the large Peshawar Club for breakfast of delicious curried prawns (which had come up packed-in ice from Karachi or Bombay), sitting on a wide verandah, Regimental Band playing throughout completing their programme with "God save the King" , at which all, naturally, stood up. On one occassion being joined by an Officer in full evening dress, who rose from the flower beds behind a hedge and stood strictly to attention. His party the night before had evidently been a good one.

There was also a Hunt at Risalpur run by our Brigade, which was fun, but the country was flatter and less full of hazards, than the famous P.V.H. There was a good deal of polo and rivalry between the Regimental team and the Gunners. We often stayed with friends in Peshawar and Risalpur for their polo weeks.

The British in the The Army in India were in a unique position, in that we were all approximately the same age. (One never saw an old Englishman or woman), we all had about the same amount of money and we all came from the same country and background. There was nothing to buy beyond the means of one's fellow officers. A number of the British Cavalry came from richer families and had a private income, not many Indian Cavalry Officers did. A few of the British Cavalry thought themselves slightly superior to their Indian Cavalry neighbours, when they first came out to India, making senseless remarks such as, "How you can stick this awful country I can't imagine" or "How on earth did you learn the lingo?" They resolutely refused to learn Urdu, although they were in India for at least four years. One of my British Cavalry friends said to me, on the polo ground, "You speak this language, be a dear and tell this syce of mine he has got the wrong bridle on my pony". I replied, "I certainly will not, you've been out here as long as I have, why don't you learn to speak to him in his own language yourself !" All Officers in the Indian Army were obliged to learn Hindustani, and had to employ a Munshi or Indian-teacher to learn to speak, and write it correctly. He came to the Officer's bungalow when he was off duty and was paid by him, until he had passed the examination, both written and spoken. We wives learnt the language from our husbands. It was known as 'Memsahibs Hindustani'. We never had English speaking servants as the British Cavalry did. Their servants were invariably inferior because I suppose there was less choice. The British Cavalry left most, or all, of their precious china and pictures in England, whereas we took everything we possessed out with us knowing the length of service our husbands' would have to spend in India. The result being we had more delightful looking homes, than they did, and could entertain with gracious belongings. Once a Cavalry friend from a British Regiment said, "Look at this girl, wherever she goes she makes the bungalow she's in look like England" a very nice compliment. Once they had settled down they realized that the Indian Cavalry Regiments were as good as their own. Knowing the terrain and country naturally far better than the British Soldier could and therefore nearly always out-manoeuvring them on military exercises, as they were the first to admit. We made many life long friends from British Cavalry Regiments, lasting to this day.

During my first two winters in Mardan, we lost no less than three of our officers, and one British policeman. The latter had gone out with two of his men on foot, to quell a violent riot outside Mardan, where stoning and killing was taking place. He bravely endeavoured to disperse them, but alas, was surrounded and when they dispersed his body was left lying dead. He was a fine young man, and very popular. The other tragedy occurred when the Guides Infantry were ordered by the Peshawar General to advance and capture a hill, which Mohmand tribesmen had occupied. A platoon advanced under merciless fire. Godfrey Meynell, who was commanding, continued to advance firing his revolver, until he ran out of ammunition nearing the summit. Although wounded, he continued to advance hurling rocks of defiance at the enemy, before he was killed. He was awarded a posthumous V.C. Tony Rendel who was also killed close behind him, received the unusual award of a posthumous M.C. Another Officer, Goff Hamilton, received the D.S.O. in this action and the hill was successfully taken. The dead were buried in the peaceful little churchyard at Mardan.

Godfrey was a brilliant officer and a great loss. Speaking such excellent Pushtu, that he could disguise himself as a Pathan and cross back and forth across the Frontier with impunity, gaining a great deal of tribal information in the process.

Our third very sad loss was Colonel Pat Grant, a most delightful Scot, with a tremendous sense of dry humour and the kindest heart. He was hit in the head by a sniper's bullet, when commanding the Guides on one of the many 'sorties' from Mardan and also lies in the graveyard there.

As the weather in Mardan got warmer after February, we had to resort to mosquito nets and before we left for the hills it became too hot to sleep indoors and we had to have our beds put out on the lawn, or on the flat roof.

There was something tremendously fascinating in sleeping outside, under a clear night sky studded with myriads of stars, like gold dust above us and then to hear the Bearer at 5 am carrying a hurricane bhutti waking my husband up saying quietly, "Sahib, sahib char te-ar hi", (your tea is ready) and a sleepy officer would tumble out of bed and go indoors to dress for early parade, while I lay awake listening to the distant sounds from the Bazaar. Sometimes 'tumtums' would be beating and always the jackals shrieking in melancholy reply. Later I would have my chola hazri (early morning tea) and then I would go for my early morning hack, returning at 9 a.m. when the Sahib came back to our Burra (large) Hazri - a full English breakfast. After this Reggie went off to "stables". This consisted of strolling down the lines of tethered horses in his squadron, inspecting the condition of the horses, their stables, shoeing, and general well-being. We always had our own Regimental farriers, or mistris. One of ours was a very gifted man and could copy, in metals, almost anything you asked of him. On one occasion I asked him if he could copy a large Georgian salt cellar and spoon we had. He did it so meticulously, including the dents and the silver hall mark, that to this day I do not know which is which.

There was one occasion which caused much hilarity, when a very high ranking Cavalry Officer was inspecting the Risalpur Brigade to which we belonged and duly arrived in Mardan with his full staff in attendance, to inspect the Guides cavalry. He took hours peering into every nook and cranny, horses feet and even their feed bins examined. These were galvanised tubs on a long line of mud built feeding troughs all the horses being tethered and protected from the sun by straw matting roofs. Needless to say for this great day of inspection by the 'Burra General Sahib' everything was immaculate. The Union Jack flying, the Quarter Guard in full dress at attention and the Officers particularly well turned out, following his cavalcade. The General, never one to overlook any slackness, decided to taste some of the horses fodder from the feed bins, covered appetizingly with bran. After eating from the third horse's meal, apparently with relish, the Sergeant Major in attendance stepped smartly forward, saluted and said, "Beg pardon Sir, them's be rat droppings you're eating". The pace of the inspection accelerated sharply from then on.

On another review a visiting Infantry General arrived to inspect the Regiment and decided to mount his charger at the Quarter Guard who were standing strictly to attention with pennants flying. He had a very large horse and he was a very fat man, so he told the Adjutant to give him a leg up. The Adjutant stepped smartly forward and performed his duty with such diligence that the General shot straight over his horse and landed on his bottom on the other side. The Adjutant and Quarter Guard stood strictly to attention and never even smiled. I will not describe how much mirth took place that night in the Mess.

There was much to laugh at in those carefree days of the early thirties, among friends in a superb climate, but I think many of us, particularly the women, turned our thoughts towards England, and wondered when ever we should get back. We looked forward to the day when our husbands would retire and we would be in our own country again.

Chapter Four

'There's a boy across the river with a bottom like a
peach but alas, I cannot swim'
(English translation of the first lines of an old Pathan love song)

Pathans

The Guides Cavalry was made up of one Squadron of Dogras, one Squadron of Sikhs, and the third and Headquarters Squadrons mainly of Pathans. This included Yuzafzais , Akora and Saghri Khattacks, very handsome men with thick black hair, cut in a bob and tucked behind their ears. Needless to say, clean and oiled, as most Indians have lovely hair and all the better classes keep it immaculate. These men were well over six feet tall, and their famous Khattack or war dance, whirling naked swords over and around their heads, spinning as they circled faster and faster, was both spectacular and graceful. They gave this dance, the night before they left for Active Service in the Middle East in the last war, carrying flaming torches in their left hands. Very inspiring and warlike it was.

In the early 1930's a strong local rebellion led by a fanatical character from across the border known as the Faqir of Ipi, became violently anti-British. He formed an Army who wore red uniforms and 'Sam Browne' belts, which were in fact originally designed by the famous General Sir Sam Browne, V.C. of the Guides. These rebels were also armed with rifles and became a sore trial to the Indian Army. Their cry of Inkelab, Zingibad, "Down with the British.", could be clearly and regularly, heard from our bungalow by the river, where they marched on the other Bank. They created havoc along the Frontier, killing and pillaging as they went. I remember some crossing the river, and climbing on the gates of our bungalow, screaming threats and abuse, and we women and children had to remain locked in our bungalows until they were seen off . They were known as the red shirts or revolutionaries. One spring Reggie was driving us to Nowshera to catch the Frontier Mail for Bombay and England, when ahead of us we saw that a large band of these Red Shirts had formed a blockade across the road at a very notorious village known as Takht-i-Bhai. He said to me, "On no account must we be stopped, so keep your hand pressed on the horn". He pointed his loaded revolver ahead, and with his foot pressed full on the accelerator and his left hand on the wheel, he charged at them full speed. Luckily for us they sprang aside, and we sped through them, but it was a tense moment. They were a merciless crowd, and a very real danger. The Political Officer of the District, an ex-Guide named Barnes, who lived alone, in a village very near the border, had a squadron of the Guides (my husband's) to protect him throughout that summer. He had had many shots through the doors and windows of his Bungalow, but would very bravely walk abroad unarmed, allowing the villagers to approach him and hand him petitions for justice, over some local quarrel, as was the custom. On one occasion, a Pathan handed him a petition with his left hand, and as Barny took it, brought his right hand from behind his back and fired a pistol point blank at his head, missing it by a tenth of an inch. Unfortunately for him, Barny was a rugger blue, and brought him down with an immediate tackle. He was summerarily tried for attempted murder, and hanged that night on a nearby tree . Justice was prompt on the Frontier. Alas, this brave officer was killed by a similar ruse in Baluchistan, a few years later.

The Guides Officers always wore Khaki breaches, and topies when playing polo, for a rather remarkable reason. In the early part of the century they were holding a fort on the frontier border and, as usual had made a polo ground outside the fort. An invading armed force of tribesmen swarmed over the adjacent hills unseen, but watching the 'Sahibs' at their sport. They sent an armed messenger forward to warn them that they could finish their game, but directly they returned to the Fort it would be attacked. This somewhat chivalrous gesture, was put into effect leaving the white garbed officer easy targets from the hills for the hidden men among the rocks were dressed, as always, in their dust coloured clothes. This resulted in heavy casualties to the Guides. The Commanding Officer ordered that ever after that day all Guides Officers would wear khaki (a Persian word meaning dust coloured) whenever and wherever they played polo. 'Khaki' also was invented by the founder of the Guides, Sir Harry Lumsden. It was in fact the Guides who wore the first khaki uniforms when originally raised , a colour which eventually became universal in the Army.

The Pathan was a strange mixture of chivalry and terrible cruelty, mutilating their foes on the battlefield most horribly, thus making it essential to collect the dead, and wounded, before any retreat. The British and Pathans had a strange respect for each other, a relationship in which each admired the other's courage, fortitude and sense of humour. They had much in common, except perhaps, in the matter of sex. My husband never would tell me the rest of that Pathan love song!

It should be realised that we lived in a far Northern station far from cities and their amenities. It was lucky that most of us were young and healthy, as the nearest hospital was the Military Hospital at Peshawar forty odd miles away. I personally was always aware of the risks my children were in from snake, scorpion or centipede stings, and all the diseases prevelant in India, such as cholera, smallpox and even plague. We were all inoculated against these illnesses, but there was rabies too, and dyptheria to think of. For young children there was also the mosquitoes with their risk of malaria, as well as sandflies, which could cause a very high temperature indeed, known as sandfly fever. So fly sprays and citronella oil were constantly in use. We even had all the vegetables washed in pinky pani (permanganate of potash), before they were cooked, and this had to be seen to be done. Of course all our drinking water, and milk, was boiled.

We were, after all, strangers in a foreign land, and the natives of India had acquired a certain immunity to these illnesses I speak of. They dwelt round the village pond in their mud huts, which harboured multitudes of mosquitoes, and many Indians suffered from Malaria, and I'm afraid very many other diseases too. But the climate, sparkling air and sunlight on the North West Frontier seemed to make their rural life a happy one. The men tilling the barren land, with their primitive wooden implements, and drawing water from a well with a skeleton cow or water buffalo, harnessed blindfold to a creaking wheel bringing buckets of water up to irrigate their meager crops. The women, meanwhile, squatted round a charcoal fire kneading wet dung pats with which they plastered the walls of their huts, to dry in the sun for winter fuel so depriving the land of the manure it was parched for. A vicious circle, as they needed heat in the bitter winter months and there was no foliage or timber to fell. Despite the hardship of their lives, they always looked happy, and laughed a lot. Their children were well fed - if dirty - and they greeted one with smiles and salaams. Only the children begged as one rode by, generally shrieking with laughter in the process.

Each village had a fearsome pack of pi dogs (mongrels), largely as guard dogs. They were mangy and vicious and would pursue one on horseback until out of range. As we would generally have our own dogs with us when hacking, we gave the villages a wide berth. Most of these pi dogs were infected with rabies. I remember a friend coming round to my bungalow, when our husbands were away, and asking me to come and look at their pony who was behaving quite madly. This I did, and was horrified to find it covered with blood, and rushing against the walls of its stable. We persuaded its unfortunate syce to take it to the Regimental Vet, little realising the danger we were subjecting him to, as it snatched off his pugaree several times on the way. The Vet realised immediately that it was mad with rabies and it was shot forthwith. It had been bitten in the hind foot by one of these rabid dogs.

In all my time with my husband's Regiment in Mardan we never met the wives of the Indian V.C.Os. (Viceroys Commissioned Officers) on any occasion, either Military or Social, for the very good reason that they were in Purdah, and their husbands would not allow us to. They themselves would entertain us in their Mess for a Tamasha or special occasion, being most hospitable hosts, and we would ask them to our homes, but never their wives. In fact, it was explained to me that I must never ask a Risaldar-Major (somewhat equivalent to Regimental-Sergeant Major) if his wife was well, instead I should say I hoped his family was well, or say his butchas (children), but never mention his wife. When Reggie became Commanding Officer in 1939 I then asked if I might visit the Indian Officers wives. It is necessary to explain that at that time all Indian Officers were known as Viceroy Commissioned Officers, and were not officers commissioned by the King Emperor. Good V.C.O.'s helped to make a Regiment, and were an essential link between the British Officers and the soldiers.

A tremendous spirit of loyalty and affection existed between the British and Indian Officers. It is not too strong to say a love. They really were like brothers and the breaking up of this tie is part of the sadness I feel about India. It was a unique relationship of which I know no parallel. It is true that we were in their country as rulers, but the Indian Army was paid by the Government of India to keep order and peace, which, jointly with the British Regiments, they did, successfully, for so many years. It is not, I think, generally appreciated by the present generation with its talk of Colonization and Imperialism, that as a Nation, we British in India did not seek to usurp their land and establish our homes in their country, nor interfere with their women and religions. We did produce law and order and, above all, I think Justice. Also canals, irrigation, transport, railways, grass farms, and protection from outside marauders, as well as medicine and hospitals, whilst in no way interfering with their own way of life.

Our religion was never forced upon them, nor did we try to alter theirs. The only missionaries I encountered were medical ones, who did unbelievable good and sacrificed their lives in dangerous, and remote areas in the task. A perfect example is the late Sir Henry Holland a brilliant eye specialist, who could have made his fortune in Harley Street, but preferred to stay on the Frontier of India, operating on up to one hundred patients a day. They trekked for many miles from over the Frontier to find the magical Doctor Sahib in Quetta, who would give them back their sight for nothing. Blindness from cataract was universal in the dust and glare of the barren hills of the Frontier.

When Reggie was Commanding I did manage to visit our Indian Officers wives in their homes regularly. But I found them so terribly shy and unable to speak, leaving their husbands to answer my questions. I asked if I could talk to them alone, otherwise they stood in the corner of the room, often holding their sari across their face, whilst I made strained conversation with their spouse. Eventually I got my way, and met the women alone, but they were so incredibly young, about fourteen years old upwards, and simply educated, that it was an uphill task to get on terms with them. They were so tiny and gentle, that I must have seemed a terrifying female to them, and I had to persuade them to sit down beside me and admire their saris and jewellery, generally bangles and nose rings. Eventually one got some shy giggles and a response. I did once persuade our Risaldar Major to allow his wife to come to tea with me, and see my children and home but he agreed only on condition that I sent all my male servants out of the house and compound and not even my husband could be present. This sort of situation is so difficult for people in England to understand. Now that at last emancipation has come to the upper class women of India.

Life on the Frontier in those days still held a lot of its ancient past, as an incident in the first world war illustrates. The Guides Infantry had been ordered overseas on active service and the usual war-like festive party took place on the night before their departure. One of the Pathan Officers, who was not among those due to embark, taunted his Subedar-Major by saying, "You will see what is going to happen to your wife when you have gone". This was an intolerable insult to a Pathan which could only be answered by death. The Pathan Subedar leapt to his feet and stabbed the man and then fled across the Border, beyond the power of British law. The Regiment had to sail without him, meaning desertion in the face of the enemy apart from murder, for which the penalty was death. He was therefore an outlaw and always fearful of capture. He was a fine man, and soldier, and by his code had acted correctly and honourably. Years after the war was over he sent petitions to the British Raj by devious means, for pardon, and the chance to return to his home. Messages were exchanged secretly between him and two British Officers in the Guides, who eventually had a clandestine meeting with him on the border, and hid him on the floor of their car, covered him with blankets. They drove straight to Government House, Peshawar, and asked to see the Governor, pleading with him that the man was not a villain, and surely by now, had earned pardon after his banishment for so very many years. He longed to be a free man once again. The Governor said, "where is he?" and when they replied "Outside in our car" he looked at his watch and said "I'll give you one hour to get him back across the Frontier, or I'll arrest you all, and please remember that this conversation never took place !" I am glad to be able to end this story with the fact that he was eventually allowed to return and stand trial, which he did, in my day and was given a very light sentence in jail, and then a free pardon to spend his remaining years in his own home village near Mardan.

The Guides Cavalry was posted to Bannu, in 1933 in Waziristan. It was the first time the Corps had been separated since it was raised in 1845, except when, on Active Service, in the first World War and other frontier stations. Promotions in those days were very slow, the Commanding Officer would serve in that capacity for five years. Far too long, and the retiring age was 52. An Officers' pay in the 1930's was extremely low, so it was recognised that an officer should be allowed to leave his regiment periodically to take a job on a Governor's staff, or perhaps be seconded to an Indian State for two or three years which gave him extra pay. Or, if he was P.S.C. (passed staff college), he would go off on a staff job to G.H.Q. at Delhi. Strangely enough those officers who did pass the

Staff College examinations were inclined to be looked upon with a certain derision, rather like book worms or clerks, as opposed to fighting soldiers. Very few officers attempted to even take the exam. All they wanted was to serve their Regiment, get command of it and retire at the end of that command and go home to England their own beloved land. Home leave was something tremendous to look forward to. It came every three years, with eight glorious months in England again. As our ship drew near to the white cliffs of Dover, we became happier and happier. To see only white faces, our own kindred again and to be welcomed home by my parents and old friends and relatives and to show the children all the wonderful things in England, was bliss. Even the cows and sheep and chickens were double the size. It is impossible to describe how beautiful England looks when one has been away for years in the East. The colours of the fields and trees are breathtaking, and all the small gardens, full of flowers, near the railway line as one speeds towards London, stagger one with their neatness and colour.

All these things one took for granted before leaving to live away from them. It was, I think, in retrospect, a very big step to marry a man in the Indian Army. One had to realize that one would be domiciled in India (not just anywhere) for up to the next twenty years of ones life. Separated from family, and home, and then later, one's own children who had to stay in England at school. Life in the Indian Army was one long separation.

Before the war it was regarded as essential that all British children over the age of six should not stay on in India, because of both the climate and lack of schooling. So many children, Rudyard Kipling being a perfect example, were deprived of their parents love and encouragement, just when they needed it most, being left with aged grandparents, elderly aunts or in harsh boarding schools. Thus being deprived of the closeness and love of their own parents when they were so young. It is difficult today to realise just how very far away India was from England at that time, with none of the paid fares and air transport existing today. An officer only had the cost of three first class return voyages for himself and family during his service in

India, which could be anything up to thirty years. So voyages home had to be used with care and travel by tourist class, as it was called, the only way to eke out the money which the Government provided and thus gain an extra trip or two without delving into one's own pocket. I was in England when the Guides Cavalry were sent to Bunnu in Waziristan. I sailed back to join my husband six months pregnant, leaving my little boy with my mother. I thought it was a ghastly place, bleak and rocky. The Cantonment was surrounded by barbed wire and we were still harassed by the elusive Faqir of Ipi and his terrorist followers. In fact I had to have no less than five armed orderlies to accompany me on my morning rides. On top of this Reggie was sent away to an outpost called Wana where we had a Squadron near Razmak. No white women were allowed there. Thank heaven we had booked an English Maternity nurse from the famous pool of Minto Nursing Sisters based in Delhi for my baby's arrival. An ex Vicreine Lady Minto had formed this organisation for English women in isolated stations, and they were a band of wonderful nurses. Highly trained and efficient, they would set off for anywhere in the blue, to nurse and help women whose husbands were posted to far flung parts of the Indian continent. As the army doctor, who was to deliver my baby, was posted to another station three days before the baby arrived, I cannot think what I should have done without Sister Agnes.

Our bungalow was fairly primitive, with only mud baked floors covered with Chittai (rush matting) and we had no running water in the house, so it was not an ideal place to give birth. But she coped calmly with everything. My husband came back and my baby girl was born. I was twenty three. I cannot say anything good about Bannu and disliked our two and a half years there. We went on home leave whilst there, and brought back the two children and nanny, before thankfully being sent back to Mardan. Funnily enough, of the only three Regiments stationed in that harsh and barren place, their Commanding Officers' names were Blood, Gore and Savage, which I think aptly describes it! There were constant alarms and forays into the barren hills to capture raiding Baluchi tribesmen.

I was lucky enough to have a wonderful English Nanny for twenty years. She had replaced old Nana who had had to retire, and this one we dearly loved. Her name was Ellen Bunn so she was known as Bunny. She very rarely got angry but on an occasion when she did, my youngest son christened her "The Hot Cross Bun"! It must have been lonely for her, as only a few people had English Nannies on the Frontier, so she had few chums, but she was full of fun and always interested in our different surroundings and travels. She had never been to India and found the Himalayan scenery, camel caravans and bazaars, fascinating. She was in her late forties but had a great urge to ride, so my husband had the quietest horse, in our stable of nine or ten ponies, well exercised on Nannies afternoon off, and brought to the door by a mounted orderly and off she set happily on a leading rein with her escort. It gave her immense pleasure, and solved the problem.

Chapter Five

"He also serves who only stands and waits"

Indian Servants

Like everyone else in our situation it was impossible in those days to do without a large staff of Indian servants. We were expected to maintain a standard of living befitting an Officer in a Cavalry Regiment and in any case, no Indian Servants would have worked for us, unless we had maintained the expected number of men, each for his specific job. The Bearer, or head man, would not dream of sweeping the floor for which a sweeper was employed. He invariably created a great deal of dust with his witches broom, which settled over everything, and the Bearer came after him and dusted it all off on to the floor again. This happened twice a day!

The Khitmagar would not consider butlering unless he had an assistant Masalchee, or pantry boy, the Khansama or cook, would not do the cooking unless he had his 'mate' to do his chores. If one had a nursery and children, with an English Nanny it was obligatory to have a Nursery Boy exclusively in attendance on the Nurse Misssahib. If there was a garden, as we all had, the Mali (gardener) had to have a coolie to help him. It was an order that every officer must keep a charger, and travel 1st class on the railway. All of us kept horses, so each had to have his own 'Syce' or groom. As we had no running water taps in the bungalow for our water supply, we had to have a Bhisti (water carrier) who would carry a water filled goatskin on his back, and bring this to the house. His job was also to fill the large jugs in our bathrooms, and the earthenware chutti on the floor, for our baths. He also heated the bath water outside, in old Kerosene oil tins, on a charcoal fire, which he would pour into our tin tubs when called for. The sweeper, who came from the untouchable class of Hindus, had to clean out the commodes, known irreverently as thunder boxes.

This was the essential staff living in go-downs, small mud huts in our compound or garden precincts. Apart from these, we employed a Dohbie (washerman) who came weekly with his donkey and for a monthly wage, took all our washing away and bashed it clean on a rock in a nearby river, ironed it meticulously with a heavy iron holding red hot charcoal inside, and brought it back the following week, beautifully starched. This included stiff shirt fronts and collars, white ties and waistcoats, as well as glass cloths and dirty dusters. I always thought they were the most overworked and underpaid of any of the servants, giving this service to several bungalows as they did.

Then there was the Derzi. He also came from outside, on a bicycle, carrying his singer sewing machine on the handle bars. He would spread his rug on the verandah, sit on it with his legs folded under him like a Bhudda. He worked meticulously, with materials one had bought in the Bazaar and proceed to copy anything one gave him. Children's clothes which they had grown out of and could not of course be replaced. There were no shops to buy them from!

All these people became one's responsibility. If he or his children were ill we saw they were paid and if possible persuaded him to come to his native hospital. If the injury was minor, we would doctor him ourselves. We were, in fact, an extraordinarily united little community. They very rarely let us down, They were paid the nirrick (correct) wage for their job, and, with their fairly light work, whilst living with their families, they appeared to be a very contented and certainly a very loyal staff. When they left they asked for a chitty, reference, which they treasured as an insurance to show to their future employer. I read one which said "This man is a very light fingered worker". A mean trick I thought, as the applicant produced it with pride, unaware of the innuendo.

As Reggie rose in rank so did my Izzat, position of importance, which reflected on the servants we employed. It is to their credit that in 1942, when he was commanding the Guides Cavalry in Quetta, and they left for the Middle East on Active Service, not one of my servants deserted me during the four years I was a 'grass widow' (Army wife separated from her husband by war or excercises) in India. They moved with me when I had to vacate my Colonel Sahibs spacious bungalow and move into quickly erected mud huts for abandoned wives. We renamed ourselves abandoned women! Later when I moved right across India to Dehra Dun at the foot hills of the Eastern Himalayas, they came too and stayed until I left India for good in 1945. I consider the honesty, faithfulness and kindness I had from them quite outstanding and I hold memories of real affection for them. I owe them a debt of gratitude I can never repay, but shall always remember. They never stole from an employer who treated them fairly, having their own code of honour in this respect. An example was when one summer I took my Pathan bearer to Kashmir and he not only knifed a friend's bearer for some insult but he also stole the hotel crockery and cutlery. I was summoned by the Hotelier, Mr. Nedou, to his office and told I must send the bearer back to the plains forthwith. When I spoke to Birket Shah of the sharam (shame) he had brought upon me, he looked astonished and said "But I was not stealing the Memsahib's belongings, this I would never do, I was only taking the Hotel spoons, that is not stealing".

The Khansama or cook, would arrive at my desk punctually every morning, to get his menu ordered for the following day, and produce his account for the previous one. He did all the shopping in the Bazaar for the fresh food, and the Memsahib handed out from her store cupboard what he required for the following day's meals. This was kept locked but if he demanded more sugar, cooking fat flour etc., than I had portioned out, I invariably gave it to him. No doubt it was too much, but it was one of his perks and I felt that if I was too strict about this I would get a bad meal in consequence. It was accepted that he received one anna per person, for soup, ridiculously cheap when they managed to produce the best consommé I have ever tasted.

The Bobajee Khana (kitchen) as it was always called, was separate from the house by quite a distance and this I carefully inspected every day. Contrary to accounts I have read in other books on India, they kept their Dekshis (saucepans without handles) spotlessly clean and did most of their cooking and washing upon the floor with a mud made charcoal oven to cook on. How they managed to produce the delicious meals they did in these conditions is amazing. Having prepared the dinner, it was carried over to the pantry, by the Masalchi, (Pantry boy) and placed in a most ingenious device known as a Hot Case. This consisted of a large wooden crate standing on end and lined with hammered out kerosene oil tins. A very hot charcoal brazier at the bottom, regularly fanned, kept the food, on barred shelves above, perfectly hot, whatever time one chose to call for dinner. Very often we told him there would be two or three extra sahibs coming, but miraculously there was always enough. Some Memsahibs chose to cut the cooks bill if she thought the previous nights dinner was not up to standard. I never once did this and looking back how glad I am I didn't. Having to cook myself now, and finding that the best dishes I can make sometimes go wrong, I should be furious if someone cut me for the ingredients I'd paid for! If crockery or cutlery was short in one house hold it was quite usual for the Khitmagar (Butler) to borrow some from ones friends so if a big dinner party was given, we often found that we were eating off our own plates in someone else's house. I know that this was common practice in Calcutta, where very large dinner parties were given.

My mother told me once she had a dinner party for twenty but had only nineteen very precious cut glass finger bowls. The Indians called them Bowly glasses. A colossal crash was heard outside by the guest and the Khitmagar came in and whispered anxiously to my father that there had been an accident outside and all the bowly glasses had been smashed. My mother suppressed her displeasure, only to be told that she need not worry, not one had been broken, but as there were not enough to go round, he had told the Masalchi to smash some empty bottles on the floor, and so save face for the Sahib and Memsahib.

All our head indoor servants, Bearer, Khitmagar and Nursery boy wore a uniform of white. The waistcoat was scarlet with a gold coloured monogram of GC (Guides Cavalry) embroidered on the chest, as well as on the scarlet band across his white puggaree. Each winter they were given a thick serge tunic buttoning up to the neck band and made to measure by our local derzi and given to them for keeps. As also were warm jerseys to wear under them on the Frontier. They always looked immaculately smart and clean and served a meal with the highest quiet efficiency as one could get anywhere in the world. Barefoot always.

They were devoted to children, and would spoil an English child abominably. I am glad that I never had an Ayah for mine and was lucky enough to have my English nanny for twenty years. We always insisted that our children behaved politely to all the servants. I remember once in the war years, when I was away my little girl of ten saw the bearers children playing in my drawing room. She told him he was a soor-ke-butcha having no idea what it meant. It was in fact "son of a pig" and a terrible insult to an Indian. He arrived at my desk after my return and politely salaamed and then told me the Missisahib had insulted him with these words. I called her in at once and asked her if she had in fact said this. When she said she had I told her to stand in front of 'Sherriff' and beg his pardon at once. This she did, and he salaamed her with great dignity and went out. I only mention this small episode, to make my point that we did not treat Indians with discourtesy in the Indian Army.

Chapter Six

'My name is Jonathan Nathaniel Curzon I am a very superior person. My cheeks are pink, my hair is sleek, I dine at Blenheim once a week.'

Snobbery and Protocol

Composed by some wag of the then Viceroy of India. A good deal of the Protocol that existed in India in the 1930's somewhat surprised me. Not much of it existed on the N.W.F., where we had a Governor only in Peshawar. But it was obligatory to sign one's name in his Book and invitations to Government House were expected to be accepted. In other parts of India the Governors and their wives were very formal indeed. The women guests had to wear long white gloves, the Civilian men white ties, and Officers wore Mess Kit and medals. We were lined up in a row before the regal pair arrived and introduced in turn to their Excellencies by the A.D.C. The women curtseying and the men bowing, as to Royalty. The delicate operation of seating at dinner was a highly important part of the ceremonial evening. Woe betide a luckless A.D.C. if he placed any wife in a junior seat than her husband's position entitled her to. I had the somewhat daunting experience of having to have the Governor of the N.W.F.P, and his wife to dine, when I was only twenty two, as by chance, my husband was the most senior officer in Mardan at the time.

Whether I, or the servants, were more agitated I do not know, when two large Rolls Royces swept up to our front door, with Union Jack pennants flying. The then charming Governor's wife, Lady Cunningham put me at my ease, by saying, "I do hope you are not worried at having to entertain us, when my husband retires, I shall be carrying my own shopping basket like everyone else in England and probably on a bicycle." But there were few like her, I am afraid.

Later, that winter, my husband was detailed to take his Squadron as Bodyguard to accompany the Governor, Sir George Cunningham, on his District tour, 'showing the flag', as it was called, and to my delight I was also invited.

H.E. (His Excellency) rode from one village to another on the Frontier holding 'Durbars' at each, when all petitions and feuds were brought before him to judge His word was accepted as law. We had two camps, which leap frogged as it were, so that having left one luxurious camp, and ridden all day, at our next destination, there was a dual one with hot baths, drinks and a delicious dinner awaiting us.

The Indian Civil Service (I.C.S.), known as the Heaven Born, were apt to put on a great deal of side, having achieved their positions by birth and brains. A large percentage of them came from Eton and other famous public schools. Judges and lawyers were a law unto themselves, and nowhere could the law of Britain have acted more successfully, and meted out their edicts with such justice and incorruptibility. Then there were the Political Agents to administer the law, over wide areas, in Provinces all over India. They were responsible for local justice. Most of them were Army Officers, who had transferred to the Civil Service, wooed by the increase in pay.

There were a host of Government Departments run by the British. Grass Farms, Canals and Irrigation and Railways whose efficiency was first class. There was too a very large forest department whose British Managers and their wives lived solitary lives deep in the jungles of India. But we, in the Army, led totally separate lives and rarely met. The business men in Calcutta, Bombay and the other large cities, lived different lives again, managing large Jute and Sugar mills, and making a great deal of money, as well as living in large comfortable houses, where they displayed the most generous hospitality imaginable. It was their custom to issue invitations to any Army Officers and their wives who came to the large Polo Tournaments, to stay with them for a fortnight or more, generally never having met them. For some reason they were somewhat patronisingly called Box Wallahs, in other words merchants. The stupidity of this attitude was proved in the Second World War, when they left their lucrative jobs, wives and children, and joined the Indian Army Regiments to fight. They have retained their attachment to these Regiments to this day, gaining many decorations, and making life long friends.

All the large Banks had British Managers. The Indian Police were officered by British of a high calibre, so graft (corruption) was virtually unknown. There was no Indian Navy or Air Force in the thirties, so that any ships or aeroplanes were British made and manned.

There were also Remount Depots run by Cavalry Officers of the Indian Army, and there were several excellent private studs owned by the British, providing beautifully bred horses for those who could afford to buy them. Most Cavalry Officers owned at least one pony or charger, of his own, and would also have six or seven Regimental horses in his stable as well. For this he paid the princely sum of seven rupees eight annas (£30-33 in today's money) a month and were therefore always known as seven eighters throughout the Army.

All these various services had their allotted place in the social scale, but in my life as a British Officers' wife, whose time was spent mainly on the Frontier or in Indian States, I did not encounter as much snobbery, as one would in a smart hunting country in England! Nevertheless it existed, and was particularly prevalent at the Seat of Government in Delhi, and Simla.

The saddest community of all were the Eurasians, now known as Anglo Indians. Accepted neither by British or Indians socially. Most of them worked in subordinate positions on the railways, or serving in the big City shops. The girls were beautiful, having the large dark eyes and long black lashes of most Indians, with slender arms, and figures, which alas like many Indian women did not last past early middle age. When the American Army invaded Bengal in the 1940's they had three to four times higher pay than the British Soldiers and needing women, they gave these girls the time of their lives, lavishing money, and presents on them. At the end of the war they sailed home, leaving many of these girls with babies to rear, on very slender means. No British Officers would go out with a 'chi chi' as they were called, and British soldiers on their pay could not afford them. Nor would these girls go out with a common Tommy.

All Indians are hospitable by nature, from Maharajahs down and it was awkward to have to refuse the gifts so frequently offered to us. But it was an order that no officer should ever accept a present for himself, or his family, from an Indian and many tears were shed by our children, when the lovely toys spread out for them on the verandah at Xmas had to be returned. This happened frequently in the Indian, or Maharajahs states. One of my friends was offered a bouquet of flowers and felt that there could be no harm in accepting such a charming gift. She later found that there was a precious stone set in the middle of it, which had, of course, to be sent back. If accepted, it would be assumed that a return gift would be offered, generally in the form of quick promotion for a son, or nephew, under one's husbands' command. They, and we, knew the form, but it was always worth a try!

The British Clubs in India have caused a great deal of criticism, and, I think, misunderstanding. As far as the Frontier was concerned there were very few, I can only remember one in Peshawar and one in Rawalpindi. Certainly there was no club life for us, however, the big cities did have several, and some were very famous, such as the Bengal Club in Calcutta which was for men only. The Saturday Club in Calcutta was for men and women, as was the Tollygunge Golf Club, but no Indians were allowed to join, which caused a great deal of bitterness. However when one realizes that all the British Community in India, were in a foreign land for a large part of their lives, I do not think it unreasonable that they formed a social and relaxed meeting place where they could enjoy their own particular national way of life, after work. No Indians ever formed any Clubs of their own, which they could have done, and excluded the British. They had no need to, they were in their own country and we were not.

Our customs were different and no English women were in purdah, whilst most of theirs were. Why should the British in those days admit Indians to mixed clubs to meet and dance with their wives, when the Indians would not allow British males to meet their wives?

This particular problem was acute in the 1930's, when there were no Indian Commissioned Officers, heads of Banks, or Businesses and so Indians were therefore living a very different social life to the British.

Towards the end of that decade, matters altered considerably. England was gradually handing over the reins and many Indian men were taking over responsible positions as heads of firms and becoming Kings Commissioned Officers in the Army, but even in my time, very few Indian women emerged from Purdah, nor did one see high class ones unveiled in public. It was certainly unheard of to see an educated Indian lady dancing with a man in public. There was one occasion during the time Reggie was Military Adviser to the Southern Indian States, (of Mysore, Hyderabad and Travancore) who of course had their own Armies, and Indian officers. We frequently met their wives socially. One particular officer, who shall be nameless, (as he became Commander in Chief after partition), married a beautiful Indian girl and they went up to Ootycamund in the Nilgiri hills for their honeymoon. We happened to be there at the time. He applied to join the Ootycamund Club, and was sent an entry form to fill in. In reply the secretary wrote to him and said no Indian under the rank of Prince could be admitted. We thought this so rude and ungracious, that we immediately gave a large party with cards printed "To meet Colonel and Mrs......"and asked all the club members we knew and they all came. They were a bunch of hunting snobs! As he himself said, "Why send me an entry form, and allow me the humiliation of sending it in completed, if they proposed to black ball me?"

Chapter Seven

I knew a man from Poona
Who would infinitely sooner,
Play single handed polo
(A sort of solo polo)
Than play a single chukka,
With a Sahib who wasn't pukka'

Sport

I consider I was lucky enough to have had the chance to hunt with the three best packs in India. The P.V.H., The Ooty hounds in the Niligiris in Southern India, and the Quetta Hunt in Baluchistan. The Ooty was like Devon and Somerset country. No jumping, but very steep hills to gallop down, with often a treacherous bog at the bottom. The pace was fast and one needed a very good horse. A great many of the Field had English thoroughbreds, or Walers bred in New South Wales when the whole of Eastern Australia was known by that name. Country bred were not considered to have enough bone to be capable of standing up to the pace and country and looked down on by the regulars. There were a number of British who had retired to live in the Niligiris. I hunted my husband's Charger Cavalcade, a lovely ride and a bold horse, who was a country bred and who later unfortunately broke his neck, being a bit too bold, in a point-to-point when my husband was riding him.

I entered him, the only country bred, for the ladies Race in the Ooty point-to-point. This race was rather unique in that, at the start, we could choose to ride East or West. The course was over five miles of really stiff going to round a given point. This was in fact done in the past when Steeple Chases were first ridden round a distant church steeple with an uphill finish. To my great glee I won! We were so sad when he was killed. He had had the honour of carrying the Commander-in-Chief on his back, when inspecting the Guides. His portrait hangs in my home today.

The country we hunted over was very beautiful, soft green downland, with small woods and streams, so very like England. The hillsmen were a tribe known as Todas. Very muscular indeed. The last race of the day was the Toda race. Run at a tremendous pace barefoot up and down hill by these hardy little men.

As usual in India, we were hunting Jackal, but again sometimes found a fox. It was all great fun, and the hacking was superb, as was the climate.

Hunting in Quetta was totally different with miles and miles of open country to ride over, mostly rock hard. The obstacles here were deep curazes or nullahs to negotiate, with large cracks in the banks over treacherous ground. As often the water at the bottom proved to be a quick-sand like mud, horse and rider often sank dangerously into it. On one occasion I saw a rider gingerly descending a very steep pot-holed bank, when both he and his horse suddenly disappeared underground. He found himself standing on the floor, of a disused Indian house or hut, and rode out of the front door to the amusement of all, having fallen straight through the roof.

Again it was all such fun, delightful hunting with no wire, and few crops in that harsh and barren land. With a fast and clever horse one could generally find oneself galloping free, with an icy wind in ones face and a blue sky above and a quick kill in the open at the end. I shall always maintain that hunting in India was just as good as it is in England. Hazards and falls were plentiful and to fall at a gallop in Baluchistan really hurts! I knocked myself out in a point-to-point when my horse turned a somersault and was in hospital for three weeks.

Horses in those days really played a dominant part in our lives. No Cavalry regiments were mechanised then, so that one lived and smelt horses all one's life and polo was the great and universal game for all Cavalry soldiers. Each officer had his own Orderly or stud groom as horse master. Indians are superb horsemen, naturally balanced, and with exceptionally good hands. The horses owned and hired from the Government by Indian Cavalry Officers were of a very high standard indeed. The great polo weeks were the, Indian Cavalry Inter-Regimental Tournament in Lahore in the Punjab and the Meerut week in which British and Indian Cavalry Regiments competed for the Inter-Regimental Cup. The peak of these tournaments was the Ezra Cup, played in Calcutta during Calcutta Week in Bengal. In this tournament not only the best Regimental Teams competed, but also teams from the Argentine and Australia, as well as famous Maharajah teams such as Jodhpur, Jaipur, and Kashmir, superbly mounted with money no object.

The standard of polo at this tournament has not been surpassed. All the teams competing averaged handicaps of 16 or more points. Some players having a handicap of ten. The four Ashton brothers from Australia made a brilliant team, and so, of course, did that of Jaipur. 'Jai' himself was a high handicap player. The Indian Cavalry's Regiments, few of whom had private means, were always on the alert for a handsome sale of a good pony to one of the Maharajas after these tournaments, or even to their richer, brother officers from a British Cavalry Regiment, but the main object of it all was to get there, let alone win. Only a good team could compete. If one glances at a map, it is easy to imagine the cost of entraining ponies and syces from the North West Frontier to the Bay of Bengal. Luckily for me Reggie was a high handicap player so I was able to accompany him on these wonderful trips to Bombay, and Calcutta.

I'd loved riding and hunting all my life, and I had so much of it in the fifteen years I spent in India. Apart from point-to-points to compete in every cold weather or winter, there were jumping competitions, horse shows and gymkhanas.

The other great sport in India was pig-sticking, though not in the North. The famous Kadir Cup was contested for each year near Mhow in the South, with tremendous enthusiasm. A truly dangerous game for horse and rider. Galloping blind through high grass and bush at full speed, to get your pig, a swift four footed animal indeed. A fall might mean facing a very brave and ferocious beast ready to charge you on your feet.

I believe the Gunners won this Tournament more than any other Regiment, as one of their main stations was at Mhow, where pigs abounded. One of our friends who won this sought after trophy on a horse called 'Battleaxe' christened his newly born baby Battleaxe. Fortunately it was a boy!

Game over most parts of India was plentiful, so there was excellent shooting. In the mountain ranges close to Mardan, there were black and grey woodcock, chikor somewhat like grouse, also snipe and if lucky, markhor and the famous Maharajahs' duck shoots over the huge jheels or lakes, brought down thousands of these lovely migrating geese and duck. There was then no restriction on the hunting of big game in India, but not many soldiers could afford the time or money for beaters and camps in the jungle, far from their stations. There were a few lucky ones who were stationed in the Central Provinces and expected to go out and bag a tiger by their Regiment.

The week spent in Calcutta for the Polo Tournament was unique. So gay and glamorous. Looking back it seems like a fairy tale. There was a Ball practically every night. The Viceroys Ball was the peak of course. Each end of the ballroom were the Thrones for the Governor of Bengal and his wife, and the Viceroy and Vicereine, while all round the Ball Room were the thrones of the visiting Maharajahs, who were dressed in magnificent brocades, silk turbans, and laden with fabulous jewellery. Also most of them were exceedingly handsome men, such as the Maharaja of Patiala. When all the guests had assembled, the Governors procession walked across the floor to their thrones accompanied by a posse of Military attachés, and A,D.C.'s.

The handsome Lord Brabourne was then Governor of Bengal, and Lady Brabourne, wore the most beautiful matching set of emeralds I have ever seen. After them arrived the Viceroy with his wife, body guard and followers. A very regal pair indeed, both being over six feet tall and the Vicereine wearing jewellery and decorations. All the men wore their decorations on their colourful mess dress and we, of course, all wore our best, and most becoming ball dresses. White gloves for both sexes being de rigueur.

As the room was filled with whirling dancing couples, all young and happy in 1938, it was a lovely sight, but the end, I suppose, of a saga.

The Admiral always had his Flagship in the Harbour during Calcutta Week in which he too gave a magnificent Ball. One night we were invited to dine on board, as luckily we knew Admiral Ramsay's Commodore. It was a great experience. The night of his Ball I remember we had been invited out to dinner, but we managed to leave in time to get to the Ball. We rushed along the quay and were just about to mount the gangway steps when we looked up and saw the Admiral saying goodnight to Their Excellencies the Viceroy and Vicereine. They were just preparing to descend so we scuttled away at full speed, and went up the crew's gangway in the dark, as the Viceregal pair descended the floodlit guests' gangway.

Another Ball which remains vividly in my mind was The Go-Lightly Ball, given by the rich bachelors of Calcutta at the Tollygunge golf club. Our hosts were all dressed in knee breeches and their tail coats bore red lapels. All lighting throughout was by red candles, and the decoration was done with huge clusters of red poinsettias, red carpets leading us to the ballroom, and four Champagne Bars, under Shamiyanah, Marquees, out on the lawns, under the stars. We danced, laughed and flirted till dawn, glamorous night indeed. We called one of our polo ponies Go-lightly in its memory.

The Race Course was full every morning before breakfast, of polo players, and their wives, exercising and schooling their valuable ponies. All of us in the Army were put up in great comfort in the large houses of the Calcutta Residents. The Race Courses of Calcutta and Bombay were famous and had large trees and spacious lawns to stroll in. Racing was not encouraged in the Indian Cavalry, largely because it could lead young officers into heavy debt, and was far from incorruptible. Those Regiments who did encourage racing were known as 'Racing Swine!'

Chapter Eight

"The splendour and the squalor"

Lands of the Maharajahs

The Maharajahs of India in the days of the Raj were a fabulous collection of men, living in great luxury and pomp, in comparison to their people, who themselves placidly accepted their lot and gave their ruler complete loyalty. Naturally the Indian states varied enormously in size, and their rulers, the Maharajahs, were given the importance and respect commensurate with the size of their domains; recognised officially by the number of Cannons fired in salute, at Official and State functions with the British. Some were corrupt, but most were fine looking men and one or two excellent administrators. Nearly every one of them offered their personal Army to fight on the side of the British in both world wars. In the Summer of 1934 we had an invitation from the Maharajah of Kashmir to be his guests at his magnificent new palace (now the Lalit Grand Palace Hotel), overlooking the beautiful Dal Lake in Srinagar .

He also offered to mount my husband for the Polo season there, lasting three weeks. He had remained somewhat aloof from the British since he had figured as an innocent party in a scandalous affair in England. As a very young man, an unscrupulous Englishman appointed to look after him in Europe, staged a scene to trap him with a lady of easy virtue in his hotel bedroom, where her supposed husband found them. This man then proceeded to blackmail Maharajah Hari Singh for some time, before being discovered and brought to justice. In order to protect the Maharajah, he was given the pseudonym of Mr. A and the case filled all the newspapers in the early twenties. Not unnaturally, he was exceedingly wary of the British after this affair.

We were, therefore, very honoured to be the first British guests he had invited to stay, and his hospitality was magnanimous. My husband had five thoroughbred Hungarian ponies placed at his disposal, and we had superb fishing on his private and famous trout streams, the Kulgan and the Tricker. His A.D.C. went out early and caught trout for our lunch and when H. H. arrived with his house party, at one of his fishing lodges, we sat down, out in the open, to a superb lunch of trout grilled over charcoal braziers, constantly basted with melted butter. The most delicious way to cook trout that I know of. We each then went to our beat on the river, accompanied by a shikari and fished till sunset. The water was so well stocked that even I, a very indifferent fisherman, caught two rainbow trout, within an hour, weighing 3lbs and 4lbs respectively. The trout rivers were, as can be imagined, in magnificent surroundings, with towering mountains, some snow capped, all round the valleys. Glass clear water tumbling over the rock strewn bed of the river and nearly always brilliant sunshine and blue skies overhead.

His palace was the essence of luxury and comfort, built on three sides of a square, with velvet green lawns, and terraces towards the Lake, and two Chenar trees spreading shade under which our lunch was served. He had, of course, absolutely first class servants and cooks, and both Indian, and English, food was served. The furnishings and even the pictures, by famous contemporary British artists, had been shipped out from England.

I remember we had Lalique light shades in our bedroom and a large bathroom from Aspreys, which impressed me considerably! The Maharanee was in Purdah, so did not appear, but I was taken to the Zenana part of the Palace to meet her. She was very handsome, in a gold embroidered sari and wore many jewels. Her little son called 'Tiger' now the Maharajah, was the same age as my little boy, which gave us something to talk about, although she did not speak English. I was sitting next to His Highness at dinner one night, when I said that I had never flown. He immediately said, "In that case you must have a flight in my aeroplane tomorrow". I thought he would forget all about it, but the next day an A.D.C. came to our room, and said a car was ready to drive us to the aerodrome. So I had my first flight over some of the most beautiful country in the world. Mountains and lakes, large forests, and snows.

Polo was played every afternoon in which the Maharajahs of Jaipur and Bhopal played, and a number of British officers. The beautiful Maharanee of Coach Behar was a guest, and her sons too, the Maharajah Banja and Prince Indrapit both alas, now dead, so young. I also met the Maharajah of Jaipurs' wife, whose beauty is world famous. She was the sister of the Maharajah of Coach Behar. I recollect an amusing incident at dinner one night, when there was a large party and H.H. of Kashmir sat at the centre of the long table. Opposite him sat H.H. of Bhopal. The latter had a very garrulous American lady next to him, who was touring India and she loudly proclaimed that she had seen nearly all the Indian states but undoubtedly Kashmir was by far the most beautiful. She thought she was sitting next to her host and I saw the two Maharajahs wink at each other. It has remained in my memory as one of the most delightful experiences I have ever had.

Two years later in 1936 Reggie was appointed as Military Adviser to the Southern States of India, a very far cry indeed from the N.W.F.P. As luck would have it my brother had been posted out to the Horse Gunner Battery in Risalpur, attached to the same Brigade as the Guides, which decided my parents to sail out to India to join us all for Xmas. Unfortunately we were obliged to leave soon after they arrived.

My husband went ahead leaving me to pack up all our goods and chattels once again, and follow him with the children and Nanny. It was a somewhat trying train journey, from Nowshera to Hyderabad Deccan, taking five days cooped up in our carriage, which was alive with tiny red ants. Any morsel of food left on a table was covered with them. Swarming down the walls, in long columns, kept the children busy with the 'flit gun'. To add to the discomfort, we passed through a dense dust storm as we neared the parched land of the Deccan, so we arrived dirty dusty and tired out, to our magnificent Military Adviser's State House. This was provided with the job, with its spacious rooms, marbled floors, and fans overhead constantly turning. It was an oasis of comfort. We even had a staircase on to the roof to two extra beds and bathrooms, which enchanted the children, who had always lived in bungalows.

The garden too was on the same scale, with its two tennis courts and a large summer house. The State also provided us with five Malis (gardeners) the head being a man, the rest women. A large indoor staff was headed by a most impressive Major Domo, with a large red, upturned moustache, who ran the household with a rod of iron.

As my husband had his office and personal secretary in the house, and our pay was increased by a quarter. We felt we were indeed in clover. It was like being in a different land. No fireplace of course, in that warm climate, and totally different flowers. Canna, Bourganvillea, and Pointsettias abounded in brilliant coloured profusion and a great vine of hanging lillies, known I believe, as Angels Trumpets, climbed up the house. The garden was full of tropical trees, in which hundreds of green shrieking parakeets made their homes.

Our lives were totally different from that which we had known with our Regiment, as we had a lot of entertaining to do for the Hyderabadi Officers and their wives, as well as State functions to attend. We were even provided with a car and a driver, named Faziadin, and affectionately known to us as 'Fussy'. We had an official car, and a baby Austin.

When I was in 'Ooty' with my children, Reggie attended a somewhat hilarious Mess Guest night with the Hyderbadi officers, accompanied by Fussy, and on the way home he passed near the latter's house so told him to get out and go to bed. A very fortunate decision, as after that, he drove so close to a wall that he cut the poor little Austin in half, removing the seat in which old Fussy had been sitting!

We were in the City itself, next door in fact, to the Prince of Berah, the Heir Apparent to the Nizam of Hyderabad, then reputed to be the richest man in the world. The Nizam was a miserly eccentric, rarely seen, and always in a greasy old tarboosh. He had a horde of wives and children in his vast Palace, but did not give them the education they needed.

His two eldest sons , Azim Jah and Moussem Jah, known as Jam Jar and Marmalade Jar, were quite unsophisticated. Although grown men with beautiful aristocratic Turkish wives, they behaved like school boys, but they were most hospitable and kind, and gave very lavish parties. When Prince Azim Jah, the Heir, rode on Parade magnificently attired at the head of his Army, he had his horse's mane and tail sprinkled with gold dust, and its hooves lacquered in gold. In contrast, his father, His Exhalted Highness (H.E.H.) the Nizam, would issue grand invitations to his Palace, and give each guest one cup of tea, with a cigarette and a biscuit in each saucer, no more. It really was rather like a comic opera.

The Bazaars were fascinating, full of craftsmen with brass, steel and copper wares, beautiful silks and saris, beside open drains running in the gutter. The salesmen squatting with his wares oblivious to the stench. The sweetmeat stalls were covered with flies.

The sacred cows, laughing children dirty and half naked, the starving scavenging dogs, deformed and leprous beggars, was a scene unchanged from time immemorial. The proximity of great wealth and dire poverty, was always most apparent in the Indian States.

There was a British Army Brigade stationed eight miles out of Hyderabad, where we had a lot of friends, so polo and riding continued as usual, but the Deccan country side is stark and grim, with huge rocks piled on each other at precarious and weird angles. As if a giant had been playing a balancing game with them. The temperature was as heavy and enervating as the landscape was harsh, dotted with cactus and huge ant hills. We had to beware of scorpions, centipedes and all forms of stinging beatles, and look in our slippers each morning, before putting a toe in. We had a never ending war with white ants. These repulsive creatures will eat their way through anything and given the chance could destroy a whole house.

In a night in one of our bedrooms they had come through the wall, eaten away the back of the almirah (wardrobe) and formed huge mounds like large beehives all down the wall. The only way to exterminate them was to find the entry to their home, where lived the huge slug-like Queen Ant they were feeding and then inject it with a special poison. Indians were adept at this. Rocks abounded everywhere, our garden was full of them, and one day the children ran in and said there was a 'huge snake' where they were playing.

I came to look and to my horror it was an enormous python curled all round the rocks they were playing in. The servants killed it and its skin measured twelve feet.

One day, on my early morning hack, I found, to my delight, masses of real English mushrooms. So I went back with a basket and picked them for our luncheon party that day, which started off with a delicious mushroom omelette. I saw the leading Hyderabadi lady looking at it with consternation when handed the dish and she said to my husband, "What is this?", when he replied mushrooms, she said "they are dirty things are they not, growing on dung, I believe?" Hurried removal of first course!

Each Viceroy would pay a visit to every major Indian state during his term of office, and the turn of Hyderabad came round whilst we were there. The expense the Maharajahs went to for this great event was colossal. He was accommodated in an enormous Palace kept especially for this grand occasion (every five years), which was surrounded by a vast tented camp for all his retainers. New tarmac roads were built from the station to his residence, and on the great day red carpets laid out for his arrival by train. My husband was in attendance with medals and walked with drawn sword, directly behind Lord Linlithgow and H.E.H., rather flippantly known to us as His Exhausted Highness. Neither the six foot five inches Viceroy, nor the five foot two inches Nizam, were great conversationalists. After walking some way in silence, my husband heard the Viceroy remark, "Have you had any rain here recently, Your Exalted Majesty". The reply was "Oh yes indeed, we had a shower last year, your Excellency". One other amusing incident I remember while we were there, was the visit of Count and Countess Reventlow, the previous Barbara Hutton (the heiress to the F.W.Woolworth fortune), which coincided with the visit of Mr. Somerset Maugham. Much, I think to the latter's annoyance, who felt that some of his thunder was being stolen. He sat glowering on a sofa in the middle of the room, after lunch, as two lady guests, at a time, were taken up and introduced, to converse for five minutes, each on either side of him. He made no response whatever to ones efforts at conversation. Barbara Hutton was absolutely loaded with jewellery as she wore every precious stone she had brought on her travels, for safety from theft. She was very beautiful, with rings on all her fingers, and many ropes of pearls and bracelets. The Nizam, determined not to be outdone by this display, ordered his own shabby tin trunks of jewels to be brought up from his cellars, and displayed to his guests. It was an incredible sight as box after box of enormous rubies, emeralds, sapphires and pearls were revealed. A vast fortune of priceless jewels, which never normally saw the light of day. Gone now into the hands of the Politicians, I suppose, when all the Maharajahs were stripped of their possessions, and wealth after partition.

My husband's job also included the states of Mysore, and Travancore the South west states in India, so we paid periodic visits to them both, where we were housed in great comfort in one of the Maharajah's guest houses which were large and gracious houses in beautifully kept gardens all fully staffed of course.

Bangalore, the capital of Mysore where the Maharajah had his Palace had a delightful climate. Permanently like a warm English summer and somewhat akin to that of the Caribbean. It lay at the foot of the Nilgiri Hills and from there one had a lovely drive through bamboo jungle over undulating hills, to the Hill Station of Ootacamund. The five polo ponies we took up there for the summer to hunt, derived great benefit from the cooler air, and the free galloping downhill. Having to tuck their quarters well under them, strengthened them for the winter polo season.

The Chief Military Advisor to the Indian State Forces, General Arthur Mills, would periodically tour all his States in a private white train of his own. The first and last time I shall ever travel in such grandeur. I remember we accompanied him to Bangalore during the Dussehra Festival, which was indeed a magnificent spectacle. The whole Palace a blaze of light from small cups of oil burners, outlining it against the soft night sky, and the procession through the streets with the gentle and dignified small figure of the then Maharajah, seated in his silver and gold Howdah, on the largest and most treasured elephant in his stables, whose name was 'Kalignarg'. I went and watched this elephant being prepared for the ceremony. It took hours of time with men on ladders, painting him from trunk to tail, in artistic designs. He became quite famous in the then current film called Elephant Boy.

Ahead of the Maharajahs procession walked two real giants, each eight foot six inches tall and beside and behind him came more and more elephants, horses and camels, as well as magnificent bulls, with gilded horns and embroidered saddle cloths, pulling, decorated bullock carts.

The diminutive Maharajah was wearing magnificent jewels, over his brocaded clothes, and with bands playing, excited crowds running and cheering, it was a great sight.

Alas the phoney war was now hovering over our happiness, and I had great personal sadness as my beloved Mother died suddenly in Ootacamund having taken a house for us there for the summer. This dark cloud has saddened my memory of Southern India ever since. The first light had gone out of my life at the age of 27.

We toured Travancore after her death, and found yet another world. India was always full of surprises. Lush vegetation and forests, and the beautiful coast line of Lochin on the very Southernmost tip of India, with white sands and palm trees, was quite delightful. It was then a Matriarchal state. The throne passing from the Maharani to her eldest daughter. The local women wore a form of sarong rather than a sari and walked proud and erect and topless, with a series of chattis balanced on their heads. They looked lovely as they walked single file along the flower treed jungle roads. Naturally the Maharani was a most cultivated and emancipated lady, and charming hostess to us. It was on our return from Travancore when my husband's second in command met us with the news of Chamberlains visit to Hitler and we rejoiced like so many others, or certainly the women did.

That spring Reggie had a letter from the then Governor of Bombay, Lord Lumley¯, later Lord Scarborough, offering him the appointment as his Military Secretary. It would have been a most delightful job in every way. He was a very popular Governor and it would have been both interesting and lucrative. Our pay was so low that educating children in England was a great expense. There were no free air passages for children from the Army in those days, in fact we never went by air, it was too expensive.

Alas, for me that is, three days later came a letter from G.H.Q. telling my husband he had been appointed to command his Regiment , the Guides Cavalry. He was quite delighted and for him so was I, but it was a disappointment they came together. Such is life. By now war clouds really were gathering over Europe and I had to go back again to England with the children, while he went back to Mardan to take over command, and move the Regiment to Quetta in Baluchistan.

We said good-bye to our Hyderabadi friends with genuine sadness. They gave us a delightful garlanded farewell party and presented us with this charming ode, written by one of their gayest young cavalry officers, Towfiq Ali whom I remember with affection.

Farewell to Major Gradidge.

We have assembled in the Mess today
It's a marvellous change from barley and hay
We are drinking to night to drown our sorrow
For dear old Reggie is departing tomorrow.
He's always been good and played the game
And remained through out exactly the same
It's our misfortune to lose him so soon
To work with him was an absolute boon.
We wish him good luck where ever he may go
Whether they be friends or whether they be foe.
Your charming manners and your charming wife
May you proceed with a wonderful life
May there be fields for you afore
Not only a Colonel but General or more
You have tried your best and saved us from gloom

And fed Mohd: All with the old mushroom
That night you remember at the 2nd Lancers Mess
Your dear little car was haunches but less
When we heard of the crash next morning in dress
We put up our hands and said Reggie God bless
It was by Jove a very narrow shave
When wives are away soldiers don't always behave
One has to remember the good old saying
If you stick to it, it is always paying
Evils may befall and friends may part
Yet distance alone can not change the heart
Well Towfiq wishes you both good cheer
And drinks to your health in Champagne and Beer
Good Luck, good health be happy and gay
Cheers to you both we'll meet some day.

Chapter Nine

"Cry havoc and let slip the dogs of war"
Shakespeare

Outbreak of War

In the Summer of 1939 I was in England with my children staying with my father and my husband had taken up command of the Guides Cavalry out in India. We had arranged that should he consider War inevitable he would send me a cable in code, which meant I should sail for India as soon as I was able to get passages, bringing Nanny and our little girl if possible and leaving our son at Horris Hill, the preparatory school at which he was a boarder and now 10 years old. I was pregnant again so really thankful that dear Nanny was gladly willing to come with me.

By August it was clear to all of us that only a miracle could stop England from being involved in war once again. Trenches were being dug in Hyde Park and people were building their own Air Raid Shelters, so I was not surprised when the expected cable arrived in mid-August whilst we were in our dear little house by the sea in Norfolk.

I went straight up to London to try and arrange to travel to India to be met with officials who told me it was utterly impossible. Hundreds of other wives were doing the same thing and, according to them, I had no hope of getting away at all. All shipping dates were cancelled and chaos reigned. Very disheartened, but not defeated, I returned to Norfolk and drove my children back to my father in Beaconsfield. From there I went up to London, to Grindlays in Pall Mall, almost daily. I was trying to get three berths on any available ship sailing for India.

On September 1st, suddenly the telephone rang, offering me a four berth cabin on the "Stratheden" sailing on September 3rd from Tilbury. Of course, I accepted at once and I then telephoned to my son's Headmaster and asked him if he thought I would be right, under the circumstances, to take my son back to India, as my father was old and frail. He said "Take him with you and return him when you can. His place will be kept", so with thirty-six hours to pack and plan, we set off for London, waving a sad goodbye to my aged father and boarding the "Stratheden" on September 3rd. I'd no sooner got into our four berth cabin than a steward appeared and started painting the porthole black. I said "Does this mean War?" and he said "Yes. Mr. Chamberlain broadcast the news this morning". As soon as we were at sea, the Captain addressed us all. The majority were women and children. He told us that we were sailing with no escort and making for Gibraltar. He could not tell us plans or route after that. If allowed, he said, we would zigzag at full speed through the Mediterranean unescorted or we would await a convoy and sail round the Cape of South Africa and await our orders there.

In the meantime, we must carry our life belts with us at all times. We should not undress our children at night, except for shoes and top clothes, as submarines were known to be in the Channel and Biscay area. In fact, after we had sailed, the "Athenian, full of women and children, was sunk by a submarine in those waters. I still remember the feeling of fear, in my bunk at nights. The side of the ship seems very frail if one knows a torpedo may come through it and, with a baby five months on the way, I didn't see how I could collect two children and an elderly Nanny into one life boat, particularly as we were accommodated four decks down. We eventually reached Gibraltar safely. There was one gun in the stern pointing skywards and manned for twenty-four hours, but it seemed somewhat inadequate with no other protection.

We had a tense time awaiting our orders in Gib for two days, but suddenly the ships engines came alive and we put to sea. None of us knew where we were heading, but once again the Captain summoned us and said he had taken the tremendous decision on his own responsibility to go through the Med without waiting any longer for other ships to arrive. We all cheered him and I am sure we all prayed that night.

It was a hazardous trip, as at that stage in the war, I doubt if anyone knew how many submarines had crept into the Mediterranean. We were chased twice, once even seeing the conning tower of a submarine and had the alarming experience of hearing one distinct scraping briefly against our ship. My children remember this to the present day. The Captain went full steam ahead, twisting and turning constantly. He had been warned of the presence of two submarines at a position where the liner was due to pass that night. At the time we were not told this, but we were told not to go to bed at all, put essentials only in small bags and all the clothes possible on our children and keep our life jackets on. All preparations were made for taking to the boats in the event of the liner being hit and we continued our zigzag course at 20 knots, mercifully unmolested. At one stage an Italian aeroplane flew round and round us and our one gun pointed menacingly at it.

We were terrified it was going to bomb us but it appeared to be checking on us and flew away. The voyage was sweltering and the strict blackout precautions were continued until we reached Aden, two weeks after sailing. Of course, it was impossible to send any messages and I constantly thought of my poor husband's anxiety, as I had sent him a coded cable telling him we had embarked. In fact, he did hear the news on the wireless (as we then called it) of the sinking of a passenger ship full of women and children near England, which was in fact, the "Athenian".

We eventually arrived in Bombay to a great welcome for our gallant Commander. We were the first passenger ship through the Mediterranean after the outbreak of war. Nanny sailed on to Karachi with the two children, who all stayed at Government House there, while I went up to the Frontier to join my husband. Then with him and the whole Regiment we moved by troop train to Quetta Baluchistan on September 28th, 1939. We settled into our spacious earthquake-proof bungalow, where Nanny and the children joined us and I was able to enjoy the happiness of being together with our family in a delightful climate.

The Quetta "cold weather" was invigorating. It was very cold indeed, with bitter winds coming down from the snow-covered mountains of Afghanistan, known locally as "the Khojak", named from an icy Pass in North West Baluchistan. The barrenness of the land is mitigated by magnificent, though brief, sunsets, when the entire sky seems aglow with fire. By day the sun always seems present, although it used to snow heavily in the winter, my main memory is of unceasing sunshine.

As usual, we had a stableful of horses to exercise and school, although of course, I could take no part in this before the birth of my baby. The children had first class "Baluchi" ponies to ride with the distinctive twist they have to the points of their ears. All "Baluchi" and many country breds seem to have these ears. Polo, hunting and shooting was in full swing and the children attended the Garrison Army School as there were many British troops and families stationed in Quetta where also was the Indian Staff College. Life was full, with parties and sports and we enjoyed each moment knowing, as we did, how short a time it could last, whilst in Europe "the phoney war" dragged on.

In January 1940, I was dressing early one morning when a strange rumbling noise, like a "tube train", got louder and louder. Quite suddenly, after a frightening silence, Hell broke loose. The room rocked, pictures crashed to the floor and within seconds I was grabbing the children and tearing outside. My husband had gone on early parade, but I found the terrified servants in the garden with me, dressed as I was in only pants and bra. It lasted, I believe, only minutes, but it was intense enough to create havoc and a number of deaths in the Bazaar and nearby villages. All the Quetta shops were smashed, with medicines from the Sikh-owned chemists pouring down the road and rolls of cloth from the merchants scattered afar. It was a horrid experience. A feeling of wanting to run and nowhere to run to. We were lucky with our earthquake-proof bungalows which withstood the shock and remained upright, whatever damage took place to moveable objects inside.

We had had minor earthquakes in Mardan, when suddenly, with no wind, all the leaves fell from the trees, but I'd never experienced the absolute terror a real earthquake creates. The result of this was that I gave birth to my baby six weeks prematurely in the British Military Hospital, after being warned by the Indian Medical Service (I.M.S.) doctor I was likely to lose him. Of my three children his birth was by far the worst.

I was taken by Reggie to the B.M.F.H. in labour one evening, when I was already in great pain. Thankfully I'd engaged my own wonderful Anglo Indian nurse, as the Queen Alexandra's Imperial Military Nursing Service (Q.A.I.M.S.) would not nurse an officer's wife in childbirth. The alternative would be an Indian Ayah. With my Nurse Miall's help I got on to the Labour Ward table under tremendously bright lights where I lay haemorrhaging badly with no covering or pillow, visited by the I.M.S. Doctor periodically and accompanied at intervals throughout that appalling night by his Indian Assistant, both of whom examined me internally several times, under bright lights whilst I was in labour, with no anaesthetic.

At one stage the labour table, (a ghastly idea) was so saturated with blood, that my dear Nurse Miall helped me squat on the corner sink! I was quite sure I was dying. I'd had two children and was not without courage, but the agony of that night will remain with me for ever.

In the early hours of the following morning, having asked in vain for Reggie throughout the night, I begged the doctor to cut the baby out of me and asked him if it was dead. All he replied was "That is what we are trying to find out".

Eventually, after hours of searing pain, he was born at 9.30 a.m., a wizened little shrimp weighing 5lbs. Tears rolled down my cheeks as they put him beside my face. No-one speaks much of child birth and for some it is obviously far easier than for others. I cannot believe that there is a worse physical agony in the world than a difficult birth, and to have one in an Army Hospital with no privacy, or sympathy, is a nightmarish experience.

After his birth I was very ill for four days, running a temperature of 104, and at one stage 105. My poor husband was demented with worry when he found the doctor in charge holding his head in his hands outside my room. My husband thought I was dead.

All the reply he could get from the doctor was, "I fear puerperal fever". On the fourth night I frighteningly expelled what seemed another child and terrified I rang the bell and found my dear Sister Miall beside me. She told me to lie quite still and not dare to move, until she could contact the doctor. In due course he arrived and the "afterbirth" that he had not cleared was later taken away from my body and my temperature dropped. I was lucky not to get septicaemia.

Crude as this sounds, it is an experience that wives in far off places, married to soldiers, may have to face.

My beloved baby made up for all the Hell. He was so tiny and vulnerable, that I adored him from the moment he was born - (Not for us in those days was the happy joy of being allowed to have our husbands anywhere near us, or even within call, during birth).

My husband's responsibility for the regiment under his command was a heavy one. They were still mounted on horses, but all were awaiting mechanization with eagerness and knew that this must come before they could go on Active Service. It was essential to keep up full training and interest alive, whilst waiting to be allotted Army vehicles. As professional soldiers they were desperately anxious to get into the war and see active service. Who, then, could possibly imagine that the war would last for nearly six years?

The Indian Congress Party was becoming very vociferous and the Indian Army was an excellent target in which to infiltrate their agitators. They were responsible for some desertions in other regiments and my husband, with the help of his stalwart Sikh Risaldar-Major, had to keep a constant watch out for them in our lines. They had an excellent opportunity to seduce young Indian recruits in the Bazaars telling them not to go and fight in white man's wars. The Bazaars too were full of them spreading this form of sedition.

In the event, when it came to embarking for active service in the Middle East, every single man in the Guides Cavalry followed his officers on board ship.

It was, however, a constant menace and anxiety, to the Commanding Officer. He spent many hours of writing to, or visiting, G.H.Q. in Delhi, to persuade the "Powers that be" to mechanize his Regiment quickly. Armour was in very short supply in India at the beginning of the war, as all was sent to the British Forces in Europe, who themselves were in short supply. Two of his subalterns could not bear to wait for mechanization and pressed to be allowed to join the "Chindits" in Burma under General Wingate. This they did and fought with distinction. David Monteith was killed in a gallant action, and his brother officer, George Butler won the D.S.O.

In the meantime, intensive training for war had to go on and life continue. It was a delightful time, except for the dread of separation, at least on the women's part. Men seem to look forward to war but I know of no woman who does.

As the hot weather arrived, I and the children had to move to a cooler climate. Although Quetta is situated 6000 ft. above sea level, the Summers are very hot indeed, with searing sandstorms. It is surrounded by a range of barren, rocky hills, and has little vegetation. Sand flies and mosquitoes come into their own, so it was really necessary for women and children to take to the hills, as usual. That Summer I could get no accommodation except some tent sites, so we spent our first Summer under canvas in a small mountain retreat called Ziarat, 9000 ft. above seal level and 3000 ft. higher than Quetta. We moved up lock, stock and barrel with ponies and servants, who pitched our large Army tents among the Juniper trees, which cover the hills in Ziarat and its surroundings.

It was a delightful way to live - in clear mountain air - with the scent of the Juniper berries everywhere. Life was simple. There was nothing to do but walk on the mountain paths and bathe in the icy cold pool fed by natural spring water and attend the knitting sessions for the troops, which were held at the "Resident's" wooden house. We were near enough to Quetta to enable Reggie to drive up for the occasional weekend and life seemed very good, except for the constant thoughts of those at war and the anxiety for those one loved. Reggie brought me the news of the fall of France while I was sitting outside my tent one evening. He was a born optimist, but even he regarded this terrible news very grimly and I remember we discussed what I should do if India was invaded by Russia when he had gone. He told me to go East and make my way to America with the children, rather than attempt to get home Westwards. I looked upon this idea with some foreboding as I knew no-one to go to, but I was sure it would be the right thing to do.

As usual, my indomitable elderly Nanny thoroughly enjoyed her camping life and always found something with which to amuse the children. My new baby son had sand-fly fever very badly while we were there, running such a high temperature that I feared for his life. However, he recovered and we all went back to our "Colonels Sahibs" nice house in Quetta in the Autumn of 1941.

At long last the armoured vehicles arrived and all the men, many of whom had never even sat in anything motorised before, had to be trained to drive them, as well as fight from them.

We had the most traumatic Last Horsed Parade of the Regiment, with bands playing and pennants flying and all our beautiful horses trotted off to be slaughtered, while the band played "Should old acquaintance be forgot". It was impossible to prevent the tears as we watched them go. What a wonderful animal is the horse. Born to be wild, full of strength and power, easily able to kill a man and yet his whole life is in man's service - pulling, carrying and working for man with utter obedience and gentleness, however he is treated. So often mistreated. With the loss of the horses also went a great deal of glamour, replaced, as they were, by smelly oily armoured cars and tanks, churning out dust and noise wherever they went.

We wives suffered a feeling of guilt and frustration that we were unable to do anything towards the war effort when we read of the magnificent effort being made by our English sisters at home. We were able to take Driving and Maintenance Courses (which ultimately stood me in good stead) and also, of course, First Aid Courses, but we had little chance of putting them to practical use at that time. Some wives, whose husbands had left, joined the "Wasbees" "Women's Auxiliary Service", which staffed mobile canteens and were sent wherever required, but for those of us with children it was impossible as they could not be left. We joined the W.V.S. and I and a friend were able to contribute to the war effort in an unusual way. In Baluchistan. The Resident was called Agent to the Governor General or AGG. His wife, Lady Metcalfe, started a shop for the Viceroy's war Fund and allowed us to use part of it as a women's underclothes department. This became a tremendous success. We could not, of course, buy any clothes in Quetta, all had to be made, so we asked the most glamorous of our friends to lend us a luxury garment they had brought from

Europe and we then bought silk in the Bazaar and used a durzi to copy it. Displayed and sold in our underwear shop at a good profit. I eventually had six durzis sitting on my verandah turning out black chiffon nighties, elegant silk negligees, French knickers, Cami-knickers, luxury bed jackets galore. All sold like hot cakes and we made a very worthwhile sum for the war effort and fulfilled a need for the wives, widows and "abandoned wives", who increased in numbers as the war progressed.

The Staff College in Quetta ran shortened courses of three months and officers left after that, for active service, or staff jobs in India. The former left their wives behind in Quetta where the Army housed them in huts quickly erected in mud and wattle and consisting of four or five small rooms and bathrooms with tin tubs and an outside tap only. We disdainfully called them "Abandoned Women's Huts". I moved into one in 1941 when my husband had gone, leaving the nice garden I had made and spacious bungalow to another Colonel and his wife. It was possible to make them both cosy and attractive, primitive as they were. There were no garages or stables, so when my husband left I sold the car and "stabled" my hunter and the children's ponies in tents. With feeding troughs of hard baked mud and plenty of straw they stayed warm and fit despite the bitter winter weather, which brought snow, ice, and the Khojak wind with it.

By this time we had become worried about our elder son's education. The number of passenger ships being sunk in the Indian Ocean, where German submarines had infiltrated and were regularly sinking passenger and merchant ships with impunity, had increased to an alarming extent and we felt it too dangerous to send him back to school, Nor did I want to risk taking the whole family back to England through the minefields and submarines. Very luckily for us, the son of a Canon Tyndale-Biscoe, a Missionary in Kashmir, came back from New Zealand and joined his father in the splendid work he was doing in Srinagar, where he had founded a school for deprived and poor Kashmiri boys, giving them a free and excellent education, as well as teaching them to box, play games, climb mountains and, above all, to swim. Though nearly all of them came from houseboat homes, practically none of them were able to swim. Under his direction and training, they had rowing and swimming sports, a life saving team and they even provided the only Fire Brigade in Kashmir saving many lives. The Kashmiri homes, on the banks of the Indus, were wooden houses and they were prone to flare up like tinder boxes. His school motto was "IN All THINGS BE MEN", which his boys certainly became. His son Eric decided that as there must be many British boys caught out in India by the war. By now there were, because many children came out to join their families by themselves, risking the submarines and all the dangers of war on the way. He started this Preparatory School for boys, attached to The Kashmiri School and so we sent Roddy half way across India to join all the other new pupils at the "Sheikh Bagh Preparatory School" in Srinagar. All the principles Eric's father had applied were carried on for the English boys, who learnt to climb and swim and lead a healthy outdoor life in a good climate. Thus this problem was solved, at any rate for the next two years.

The traumatic experience of saying goodbye to my husband when he went to the war and watching the troop train fade into the distance was shared by so many women that there is no need to describe it. But I wished I had been in England and not so far from home.

Chapter Ten

Grass Widow

Before my husband left for the Middle East, he suggested that I should take on the running of the Hospital for Animals in Quetta installed by the N.S.P.C.A. and think of it as my war work. I had been so appalled by the cruelty to animals ever since I had been in India.

I took up his suggestion with alacrity and for the next three years worked with my Sikh Sub-Assistant Surgeon and several Indian medical dispensers to try and alleviate at least some of the misery suffered by the donkeys, ponies, bullocks and camels in that harsh land. Funds had to be raised by various means, as we had no official financial support.

Having by then been in India for ten years, I had learnt to curb my impetuous rage when I saw an animal being starved and beaten. In the beginning I had on several occasions, rather rashly attacked the owner, somewhat to Reggie's dismay. I realise it was an unwise thing to do on the North West Frontier and came to understand that sensitivity to an animal's suffering is rarely, if ever, found in an Indian peasant. Apart from this they themselves lead so hard a life of poverty that it is not surprising they starve their animals as well and work them until they drop.

I did have the power, as Honorary Secretary of the N.S.P.C.A. (we did not have the "Royal" appendage) to report a man to the Police for gross cruelty and they could charge and fine him, but as one Englishman said to me "Are you there to punish or to help?". I replied "Well, to help, of course" and from then on made that my "Motto". We wanted the owners of sick animals to come to us, rather than forcing them, with Police help, to attend our Hospital. All treatment and fodder was free, but fines were imposed for deliberate maltreatment, as opposed to cruelty through ignorance or misfortune.

Some of the sores on donkeys and camels, when their packs were removed, were horrific and many animals were past curing by the time they reached us. Outsiders and Police would bring in many of the worst cases and much was the wailing and resistance of many of the owners forced to leave their beasts of burden in our care, to treat and cure free, when they wished to continue to work them until they dropped dead. I devised a plan whereby if an animal was too severely wounded or ill to heal and had to be destroyed with our Humane Killer, the owner was obliged to be present and, if he wished, take the carcasses. If he was poor, or if he had lost his animal through old age or disease, we gave him 10 Rupees. If, however, the owner was rich, or had deliberately inflicted wounds on his animal, we gave him nothing. Many did inflict wounds deliberately, often with long nails, to make an animal go faster, some out of ignorance. But many injuries came from neglect. When packs were taken off camels' backs, I actually saw wounds that went straight through their backs so that you could see daylight on the other side and they were alive with maggots, so it can be imagined what suffering the animals went through. I was always present when an animal was put down, much as I hated it. Gradually the hospital began to fill. I rejoiced whenever an owner brought his animal to our Hospital voluntarily and it was rewarding to be able to return it to him with its wounds healed. It was, of course, a drop in the ocean, I know, but one prayed it might do a little good, however small.

At this time in Quetta, Russia was our enemy and a real threat to India via the borders of Baluchistan. The possibility of an invasion was ever present. Trenches were dug and lighting restricted, which was called a "brown out". The Government began building aerodromes over the border for defense and for this undertaking hired Indian contractors to remove and level the soil. They in their turn hired donkey owners to carry away the rubble and for this thousands of donkeys were needed. Any man who owned one, or fifty, donkeys was engaged and they in their turn overloaded and overworked their donkeys mercilessly to collect their daily wage.

Old donkeys, lame donkeys, ill donkeys were all grist to the mill and terrible tales came back to me of donkeys seen left dying in roadside ditches abandoned, as no longer able to stand with broken legs let alone work. I went to the A.G.G. and asked him if I could open a Dispensary on the site of each aerodrome. He referred me to the Political Agent, but said he would give his support. The Political Agent was extremely antagonistic to my suggestion. I suppose he felt the responsibility too great as I would be operating over the Frontier boundary. Many an interview and argument I had with this rather difficult man before I got his permission and we were able to open our first Dispensary. The pitiable animals we rescued had, at least, a few weeks peace and when necessary an instantaneous death.

Strangely enough I never had a single instance of trouble or ever felt in danger from these somewhat wild men. I used to explain to them exactly what I was trying to do to help their animals and in their simple way they accepted me. I still do not know why. I was quite unarmed and of, in their opinion, an inferior sex, but materialism helped them to realise that our "Magic Silent Gun" and ten rupees was better than an abandoned dying donkey in a ditch. Anyway, in its small way, it worked and we had three Dispensaries operating over the Border with Indian Pushtu speaking dispensers.

Ultimately, of course, Nazi Germany attacked Russia, who became our "Allies" and all the Aerodromes were abandoned. I was, however, able to continue to run my Quetta S.P.C.A. Hospital until I left Quetta in 1943.

My good Sikh Sub Assistant Surgeon was tragically murdered in the holocaust of Partition after I had left India. I have been told that he was beheaded by Mohammedan terrorists, only one of the many victims of the inter-religious nightmare which engulfed the whole of India after the British had left.

Life as a grass widow was really very different. I had to adjust to living in a small mud baked hut with no particular status and no Regimental help in the way of guards at night or any of the "perks" we had from the Army which made life smooth for us, such as blacksmiths, carpenters, orderlies and so on. G.H.Q. at Delhi gave us a dwelling and no more. We were allocated this accommodation officially called "Abandoned Wives Huts" on the ruling that we were entitled to it when our husbands were ordered overseas on active service, only if we remained in the station from where he had left. If, however, we moved, the Government repudiated any responsibility for us, or our welfare, unless we chose to claim a return passage to England, by Troop Ship, to which we were entitled. I remained where I was because I hoped that my husband would ultimately return to India and also because at that time a great number of Troop Ships were being sunk in the Indian Ocean and Mediterranean carrying women and children back to the land of their birth. We spent the winters in Quetta and the summers in Ziarat, where I was able to lease three "Rondavel" huts, of the African pattern, which gave us two bedrooms and a living room, and were very comfortable, in a somewhat Spartan way. Lighting was by lamps and the "kitchen" a pitched tent. It was, however, cool and the skies at night a panopy of stars and by day the sun always seemed to shine. The children were supremely happy and it was so peaceful that it seemed unbelievable that most of the world was occupied in killing each other. I remember so well one lovely night when I switched on my small wireless and out of the air came quite purely the notes of a violin - played from the Albert Hall - by Yehudi Menuhin. Nanny and I sat together, listening to this perfection in a state of almost exaltation. I have never before or since been so moved by music, which seemed to come as magic from the quiet starlit skies. It seemed, and indeed it was, miraculous, so very far away in the midst of a bloody war.

Life went on rather differently now that most of the women were grass widows and the men bachelors, or if married, with their wives far away in England. Rather naturally sex reared its slumbrous head, with many flirtations and love affairs, some gay and fleeting, and some serious and lasting. Scandals arose and many of the stories told were hilarious, but a few were tragic. Of the latter a friend of mine, whose husband was away at the war, found herself in the family way, having been kind, and perhaps over-generous, to a young man who fell deeply in love with her and was awaiting orders to go on active service. We had no "Pill" in those far off days, so if women indulged in love affairs, they took a very great risk. She was desperate after he had left and did not want to hurt her husband, so she went to the Army doctor and begged for an abortion. This he refused. She then turned to the Nuns at the Mission Hospital. As Roman Catholics, their religion forbade them to help her destroy the life of her unborn child. Surprisingly, the Mother Superior asked her when her husband had last had leave and when she told him he had had 10 days leave four months previously, she rather surprisingly said, "My child, need he know that the baby is not his?" Alas, she did not confide her misery to anyone else and believed she could not deceive the husband she truly loved, so she went at night to the Sikh Chemists and arranged a secret abortion. This went tragically wrong and she was rushed to Hospital with septicaemia, where in agony she died. A gentle and beautiful woman, who had to die so young and needlessly.

Another, a war widow, fell deeply in love with a handsome officer, whose wife was in England. He was ordered to the war, leaving her desolate, and to everyone's surprise, she married another within a month of his departure and bore him a daughter just seven months later! Other less traumatic love affairs caused a good deal of amusement.

Earthquakes in Quetta were not at all unusual. One couple decided to go off up the "Hanna Valley" above Quetta, by car one night to make love and steal back to their respective bungalows unnoticed before dawn.

A minor earthquake occurred that night and when they returned in evening dress at 5 a.m. military work parties were clearing the rubble around their homes, directed by officers who regarded them with vast amusement and many raised eyebrows.

A young Subaltern I knew well had enjoyed a very gay evening with a great deal of drink consumed, before his departure on active service. He felt so jaded when he left the party at five in the morning that he decided to bicycle up to the large swimming pool above the Staff College and sober up with a refreshing swim. This large pool was surrounded by a high corrugated tin fence and a padlocked door, which was only opened at specified hours. He parked his bicycle and full of youth and vigour scaled the fencing and nearly fell off the top with astonishment at the sight that met his gaze. His local General, stark naked, was running round the Pool, pursuing an equally nude lady slapping her bottom with gay abandon. The bright moonlight enabled him to recognise the lady in question as his Colonel's wife. Her husband had just been ordered overseas by this General. He scrambled down the fence as fast as he could and pedalled madly back to his bachelor quarters. But every bungalow in Quetta was convulsed with laughter at their breakfast that morning.

Most love affairs were very short-lived and innocuous indeed by present day standards. It would have been difficult to conduct an illicit relationship without everyone in the Cantonment knowing.

We were all protected by servants, and soldiers, and military boundaries. It would have been unsafe to go far afield unescorted at night, nor was there anywhere to go, surrounded as we were by barren hills and desert. Luckily for me I had my stalwart Nanny as my chaperone, but I did have one unwelcome experience. A senior officer friend of Reggie's suggested to him that when he left for the war, he should take over our bungalow, to which he would be entitled by rank, his wife being in England, and, as he pointed out, if he did this it would mean that I and my children could stay in it, probably until Reggie's return. We somewhat ingenuously agreed that this was a most delightful idea. The very night after Reggie's troop train had steamed off to the war, this "friend" made a passionate pass at me and assumed that I would be happy to sleep with him. I was so astonished and outraged, that I lost my temper completely and told him very bluntly what I thought of his proposal. I suppose I was unwise as he turned very unpleasant and threatened that if I mentioned the episode to a living soul, he would make it the worse for me.

I was in an impossible situation as I was sharing a house with this perfidious friend and had nowhere to go. I applied for "an abandoned wives hut" the next day and left to visit a friend in Central India in order to avoid him. I told my faithful Nanny what had taken place and left the children in her care and I was able to move us all into a hut on my return, to everyone's surprise!

I had a great admirer, who was in a high position in the Civil Service and, therefore, unable to get to the war. He was a very charming and good-looking bachelor, with a great sense of humour, so that we became great friends and fond of each other. He knew I was in love with my husband, and he was very committed to his important work for the war, so we made each other happy with gaiety and laughter, in what was an anxious world.

At this time my husband sent me a cable from the Middle East saying he had to fly to G.H.Q. in Delhi for a week on duty and suggesting I should come to meet him there.

We had not seen each other for a year, so I joyously booked a "Ladies Only" night compartment and entrained for Delhi that evening and, as usual, locked myself in for the night, whilst the jolting twisting train progressed over the "Bolan Pass" on its south east journey. At 2 a.m., it halted at a small station where there was much banging and shouting at the door of my carriage to open up. I called back, "Go away" - the reply was, "I am the Station Master. There is a very urgent message for you, Memsahib". I peered through the shutters and saw that it was indeed the "Station Master Sahib" with an important looking crimson uniformed Chaprassi beside him, so I gingerly unlocked the door, thinking, or fearing, that there was some terrible news of my husband or children.

I was greeted by a dignified salaam from the Chaprassi and a salute from the Station Master, who handed me a large sealed envelope marked on "H.M.S.", for which I had to sign, before he would allow the train to proceed. I tore the package open frantically and was hardly able to utter when I saw the contents - a most charming letter of love-poems, and ardent devotion, from my dear, and wicked, admirer - sent all the way by road to intercept my train.

As the whistle blew, doors were locked and the train jolted on its way, I lay on my bunk, convulsed with laughter. I thought it very funny, but I didn't know if Reggie would, so I didn't tell him!

The war dragged on, with my husband still soldiering in the Middle East, after two years of separation. By this time, my elder son had outgrown his Preparatory School in Kashmir and I was able to get him in to the Royal Indian Military College at Dehra Dun in the United Provinces, at the foot of the Himalayas, 36 hours railway journey away. A much tougher school for older boys, of course, and with Army training for its Indian Scholars.

At the same time, I had the disheartening news that my husband would not be returning to India, as he had been posted to the "14th Army" and would have to go direct to Burma, from Cairo, to take charge of all the Reinforcements, British, Indian and African, for General Slim's Forces embroiled in the war with Japan. It seemed pointless to remain in Quetta in the far North Western side of India - when my husband was in Burma - and so I decided to move my family to Dehra Dun, which would be near my elder son and also nearer to my husband, should he get any leave.

All my servants came with me with their wives and children, so I took my hunter and two ponies, and we all set off across India on our 36 hour train journey, which was not easy, as all the trains were full of troops being moved across India at that time.

Chapter Eleven

Dehra Dun, United Provinces,

Congress Party Headquarters

I had been able to find a large, comfortable bungalow in Dehra Dun through the help of friends and I leased it from an Indian landlord, as I knew that the Army would "wash its hands of me" when I gave up my Army quarter. We soon settled in and were very comfortable, with a large garden and shady trees. A contrast after the barrenness of Quetta.

Nanny started a Kindergarten School on our large veranda and my daughter, now 11, went to the local Convent school. We were surrounded by the towering Himalayas and the foothill jungle, with its beautiful flowering forest trees were our boundaries. As Dehra Dun is 3000 ft. above sea level, the climate is good, but becomes hot and steamy in the Summer, so we moved up to Mussoorie at 7000 ft. for the hottest months. This was an easy pony, or dandy, ride and my children continued their schooling at the dear little school I'd been at myself about 25 years previously. Even the two charming English Westahout sisters were still in command. There were no cars in Mussoorie in those days, so all excursions were on ponies, or on one's feet. The younger children were carried in a basket, called a "Kundy", on the back of a coolie.

By night we went in rickshaws pulled by five hefty hill men at a sharp jog They often raced each other, somewhat to the alarm of the occupants, and were a carefree, laughing crowd of men, though they smelt exceedingly high and nearly all of them had lice in their hair and clothing.

There were no festivities then, as the war had taken away all the men, but the magnificent mountain ranges all around us, the pure air and the distant snows, made up for a lot. Nearly all the women were grass widows with children, and we had many picnics and children's parties, which helped the loneliness. News from home was bad and I heard that my brother, who had been missing for some time in the Middle East, was a prisoner of war in Germany.

I was getting very worried at the lack of proper education for my elder son, so when a grass widow wife with no children in India suggested to me that she should take him back to England with her, I cabled Reggie at once and he agreed he must go. It was a very hard decision as the danger to shipping at that time in the war was immense.

Reggie got a few days local leave to fly to Delhi, where Roddy and I met him and we saw him off from there. Heading for England and Stowe School, in the Autumn of 1943, he was grinning and waving and calling out, "I'll see you in the Spring". My smiles turned to tears as his train pulled out and I went back to Dehra Dun, my husband to the war zone. It was six anguished weeks before I heard any news of his whereabouts and when a young Indian Telegraph boy arrived at my Bungalow at 10 p.m. at night, with the news that he'd arrived safely, I was so relieved that I gave the astonished bearer of the good news 10 Rupees, a fortune for him in those days.

The Depot of two Gurkha Battalions was situated here and many of their officers' wives had remained behind when their husbands left for the war. I remember how bitter they were when General Wingate commandeered a whole Battalion for his 1st Chindit expedition, as he took no medical supplies and, should any of the men fall by the wayside either ill or wounded, it was made clear that they would be abandoned. We all felt that ghastly as war was, no Commander had a right to order men to follow him on those conditions and should at least have been given the chance to volunteer, particularly fighting against the Japanese, who rarely took prisoners, and, when they did, maltreated them most horribly. No women admired the fanatical General Wingate in

Dehra Dun. By now the Indian Congress Party had become very strong and powerful and they had their Headquarters in Dehra Dun, so we had a good deal of "Quit India" propaganda around us and bands of men in their unbecoming "Gandhi" caps, would walk abreast down the road, forcing us on to the verge.

India was changing very rapidly. The Indian Military Academy was situated on the outskirts of the Cantonment and by now there were many Indian Commissioned Officers in the Indian Army who attended the Courses there. There was also a large contingent of American troops and a rest camp for British troops, who had come from fighting with the 14th Army and were awaiting their return to Blighty; all in Dehra Dun. These last had few amenities and I was asked by the General's wife if I would undertake furnishing, equipping and decorating a very large tin shed for these men, as a Recreation Centre. I had very great pleasure in doing this.

I was a member of the W.V.S. and my D. & M. training in Quetta now came in most usefully. I was given a Bedford Army truck and was able to drive it to Delhi and buy furnishings of all sorts there. I, and two W.V.S. friends, set about turning our stark shed into a most comfortable Club, with Indian Sisal carpeting, and easy chairs, brass tables and lamps and a large red brick chimney piece, which I designed on an English pattern and had made locally. One of my friends, an excellent artist, painted the walls with charming frescos, depicting scenes of the English countryside and we installed a Canteen, card tables and even a Billiard table, which we purloined from a disused Officers' Mess.

All in all it was a tremendous success and when the big wigs from Delhi came to open it, the General's wife accepted their fulsome congratulations with aplomb on the platform, never saying that she had not been near the place until the opening day, nor mentioning anyone who had done all the work!

However the following tribute in the local press next day was far more rewarding.

An Appreciation

After so much criticism being directed at India and the authorities in general concerning the Amenities for B.O.R's, it is a very pleasant change to be able, in our own small way, to give some well merited publicity and praise to the splendid efforts which have been made in the Dehra Dun Area just recently.

We had watched the very rapid progress of the new Canteen - in fact the speed seemed unbelievable for India - and speculation was rife as to what 'they' intended doing with such a large building.

We were not left long wondering, for on the afternoon of the 22nd December the W.V.S. Hallet Canteen was formally opened by Mrs.Cumming, wife of our very 'live wire' Area Commander.

Speaking for the Survey lads, I think their first reaction might, without exageration, be described as one of speechlessness; certainly we had known they were building a new W.V.S.canteen, we had presumed that it would be 'alright', but such a layout as met our eyes had certainly never entered our dreams.

The Ball-room and Canteen are magnificent in themselves,but the piece de res ance of the .e canteen is, without a doubt J Rest and Rec- tion Room.   The majority . us, having lived in tents for over two years, and having little where else to go but to the cinema in our free time, appreciate as much as anybody the comforts of the Rest Room, so very tastefully furnished with it's comfortable chairs and settees, the beautifully de- signed fireplace, the billiard table, and the very 'homely' murals on the wall.

To conclude, e wish to take this oppor- tunity on behalf c   the lads in this Area, to put o record our ..re thanks to all the people who worked so hard to bring this canteen into being, and also to those responsible for arranging the Sun- day evening concert and entertainment in general, not forgetting the kind ladies who 'only stand and wait'.

At this time, a remarkable man from St. Dunstans, named Sir Clutha MacKenzie, flew out from England to start, in Dehra Dun, the only Branch of St. Dunstans in India. He had been blinded himself in the First World War and was a wonderful example of courage and ability, being entirely independent. He flew unaccompanied and was able to organise and manage the "Home" as if he had full sight. He dined, and played bridge, at my house several times, and no one would ever have known that he was blind. He brought his own playing cards with pricked markings and the score he kept in his head. I helped at his "Home" when the first patients began to arrive and I shall never forget two young Englishmen, who had come straight from the fighting line. Both were blind and one had lost his arm. It was shattering to endeavour to converse, or in any way comfort, such tragedy. I did my best and asked them to come to my house if ever they felt like it. One night at 11 p.m., I heard a good deal of shuffling on the veranda and rather alarmed I called out in Hindustani, "Who is there?" To my astonishment, an English voice answered and it was these two bereft young men, who somehow had found their way in the dark, blinded as they were, to my house. It was deeply moving. I had great difficulty in acting naturally and giving them drinks, instead of bursting into tears, and kissing them both. Soon after this they were flown back to England, where I hope they have found peace.

Another incident I remember was again late at night, as I was about to go to bed. There was loud knocking on my front door, which I opened and a rather drunk American soldier lurched into the room and asked where Edith was. I told him he had come to the wrong bungalow and he replied, "Never mind, you'll do"! I should have been alarmed, or angry, but he was so funny, and so young, that I only laughed, whereupon he sat down and proceeded to tell me the story of his life and produced photographs of all his family for me to admire. Poor boy, he was so homesick. I finally called my bearer to show him the way to get home.

My husband was given 10 days Tour of Duty in Bengal, so I caught a train to Calcutta, a journey of forty hours, to meet him there, and while we were there, we met the head partner of a firm of tea merchants, who, to my joy, offered me the loan of his firm's bungalow at Shillong, in Assam. This was most wonderful news, as it meant I could move so much nearer to Reggie. I returned to Dehra Dun to prepare to pack and move again. My elation was short-lived as 10 days later, the Japanese made a lightening advance in great strength and reached a point only 60 miles from Shillong, so my husband cabled that it was too dangerous to move there and I must stay where I was. So life, and the war, dragged on, it seemed for ever.

There were a large number of thefts by night at that time in most of the bungalows near me and of course, we had no sentries or "Night Chuprassis" to guard us as in the days of peace. I was really nervous at times, and remember frequently rushing out on to the veranda in the night cracking a hunting whip when I thought I heard ominous footsteps outside my bedroom. It was amazing that we were never molested in any way, as we were quite unprotected; white women living alone in a foreign, and by now, somewhat hostile land. We had no bars on our doors, which were only covered with wire mesh against mosquitoes and other insects. I think my faithful servants were largely responsible for my security. In fact in all the fifteen years I spent in India, I had nothing stolen at all.

I had a nasty shock one morning when my cook came and asked for leave to go to a friend's funeral and when I asked him who it was, he replied "The cook in the next bungalow. I was with him last evening and he died of plague in the night"!

As India is infested with rats, plague is a very feared epidemic. Plague, unlike cholera, is not communicated by man to man, but by fleas from the bodies of sick rats. Living, as a private citizen, I had had no warning from the Military Authorities of an outbreak of plague. I hurriedly cycled to the nearest Army official, who told me that he thought I knew that an epidemic of plague had broken out and that the City was out of bounds, I had been shopping there the day before. This meant immediate inoculation for us all, from the children and Nanny, to all the servants and their families. It is a horrible inoculation and my youngest little boy was only three and a half.

Chapter Twelve

W.V.S. Canteens in the 14th Army Area

Departure

Then out of the blue, came a letter from Col. Mary Cray, of the W.V.S. in England, who represented The President, Lady Reading, asking if I would be prepared to go out to the Chittagong Area, to organize Canteens for the thousands of British Troops, on the Maynamati Ridge in Comilla. These troops had arrived from Europe to join the Re-inforcements there prior to being flown into the fighting zone in Burma under the command of General Slim of the, by then, famous 14th Army. She explained that no women welfare workers were in that area to help with amenities, which left these British troops in need of some form of comfort and relaxation before facing the battle, in a completely foreign land. She said that she needed English women to volunteer to start and organise canteens where they were able to relax in their free time. She wrote that as I had had experience with my canteen in Dehra Dun, I should be able to help them.

I was faced with a very big dilemma as, of course, my immediate desire was to go. I had however got two children to care for and we had by then decided that I should not continue to stay out in India and subject them any longer to its health hazards and lack of education. A great friend of mine, a grass widow, offered to move into my bungalow and enable me to take over this great chance to be of use, if even only to set the wheels in motion. I therefore accepted and set off for Calcutta and she moved into my bungalow and took charge. I again witnessed the nightmare of that City. The victims of war, drought and floods, were horrific and corpses lay in the gutters of the Calcutta streets. I was given free transport on a Military bomber to fly on to Chittagong and remember my terror as we flew over the Bay of Bengal in an electric storm. I was crouching on the floor beside the bombs. In 1945 I had only been in an aeroplane twice.

My husband, who was then commanding the Re-inforcements Group of the 14th Army, met me and was allowed to house me in his "Basha" at Comilla, which was, of course, absolutely wonderful for us both.

I was in W.V.S. uniform and there on an official commission. I was given my own jeep and driver to tour the "Maynamati Ridge" where there were an average of fifty thousand young men awaiting to fly into bloody war in Burma. Comilla was a dust heap of rough tracks, hardly to be called roads, and hazards and dotted along the Ridge were numerous camps of British, Indian and African soldiers, officered by British.

Each camp had a Commandant and Staff and each camp differed considerably in the effort they had made to make the soldiers' life tolerable when they were off duty. Most of the Commandants welcomed me with enthusiasm, but one or two resented my presence in a war zone and as a woman, regarded me as a nuisance to their all male organisation. From the British and Indian soldiers I got the most rewarding and overwhelming reaction imaginable. So many had been parted from their women-folk for years and the British, in particular, felt that they had left all their loved ones so far away to join "The Forgotten Army". When I met them and talked to them, it was unbelievably rewarding. The shy smiles, to loving embraces was overwhelming. The cheers and remarks like, "What's a girl like you doing out here in this dust bowl?" and "God Almighty, its a woman - and a white one" were all a bit bewildering.

Having visited every camp, each one so different from the other, I remember in particular, the Camp of the East African Rifles, whose charming British Commandant showed me round the amenities he'd made for his African men. The pride of place being a large swimming pool. As we approached this, I was slightly taken aback to be confronted with hundreds of enormous buck negroes stark naked leaping happily in and out of the water, whilst I and his staff, fully clothed, walked among them, smiling at their huge and delighted grins of greeting. This, of course, was before the days of bikinis and nude bathers, so I was a little abashed!

I set about buying yards and yards of cotton checked gingham used as "lungis" by the local inhabitants, to make curtains and table cloths for the Canteens and got willing hands to paint the wood tables and chairs to match it. Local bamboo lamp shades for the bare bulbs, sisal (rope) mats to cover the bare floors of those stark "basha" huts and soon there was a semblance of "home", with a canteen service of grills and "special" fry ups, with unusual dishes of fried bananas and pineapple. The latter growing in abundance, covering the ground in their hundreds of crested tufts, sweet corn on the cob too, was an unusual favourite, rarely seen in England in those days. Every day was 12 hours long with increasing driving through the dust and heat, but with so much rewarding co-operation.

One memorable day, my husband received a signal that Lady Louis Mountbatten would be visiting his Headquarters and to my pleasure, I too was invited to be present as W.V.S. Adviser. We sat on the side of a very hot track for two hours awaiting her arrival, cursing a bit at the unpunctuality of V.I.P.s. Then out of a dust cloud came her entourage of staff cars and from one of them jumped this elegant and remarkable woman, in her Red Cross uniform wearing immaculate make-up. She looked like someone straight from a London beauty salon, when, in fact, she had spent hours in the heat and dust touring tented hospitals. Talking to and cheering up, hundreds upon hundreds of men. Inspecting in detail every aspect of their welfare and treatment. Sparing neither herself or her staff, in her dedication to the wonderful work she did in that Eastern war zone. She got in the seat beside my husband and said

"I'm sorry I'm late - I had so much and so many, to see" and then added "Have you seen anything of Dickie recently?", referring, of course, to her husband, Lord Mountbatten, the then Supremo of South East Asia Command. A very brave and outstanding lady.

I had had a lot of trouble with my throat for some time and I found that the incessant dust made it considerably worse. Previously, in Calcutta, I'd had an acute streptococcus infection of the throat and when I was in Comilla I found that I could barely swallow. I went to see the doctor in the six hundred bedded tented camp there, which was, in fact, the largest Army Hospital and closest to the fighting line in India or Burma. I had visited the men in it, and been so moved by their stoic courage under the conditions of heat and dust. All the Queen Alexandra's Imperial Military Nursing Service (Q.A.I.M.N.S.) Sisters were English, and their dedicated doctors were re-inforced by specialists, from London.

I was therefore able to see, in his tent, a Harley Street Ear, Nose and Throat Specialist, who said, "Come into this Hospital this eve: I'll take out your tonsils in the morning or I won't vouch for the consequences. You should not be here with a throat like this". I had no choice, but I shall not forget it.

The heat in the tents in March was terrific and I remember being carried semi-conscious on a stretcher by orderlies over dusty, bumpy tracks and my head being knocked by the orderly's knees at each rough ridge we crossed. I was in a camp-bed under a mosquito net, in a tent with two Army nurses recovering from something and they were surrounded by "boy friends" all night, roaring with laughter, whilst I lay unable to speak or move and with this searing pain in my throat (I was 34 at the time) unable to sleep or drink. It was a tough experience but I survived!

The temperature in that area in March under canvas, is not very salubrious, even if you are well. I thought so much of those with amputated limbs who were there. After ten days, my husband said I must go back to India. I had by then completed the three months I'd set out to do and I knew that I must get my children back to England.

So, alas, I had to go on the long way back by rail to Calcutta and on to Dehra Dun in the U.P. to pack up for the very last time and plan to leave for good the India in which I had spent fifteen of the best years of my life. Leaving behind so much I had loved, as well as the husband who I still felt I might never see again. It was very hard.

We applied for Army passages on a trooper for England and sold all our furniture, which we were not allowed to take. We gave up our comfortable Dehra Dun bungalow and found homes for our beloved horses and dogs. I, Nanny and the two children moved up to Mussoorie to await our passages for England, with only our suitcases. We shared a friend's bungalow there, when fate once again struck a blow.

My little girl fell desperately ill with dyptheria. The local civilian doctor told me I must take her away to an isolation Hospital, which was half way down the "Kud", or mountainside, with only an Indian Ayah attendant and an Indian Sub-assistant surgeon on call. As she had a temperature of 105, I was demented. He was really a sadist and said if I remained where I was with her, I would be a menace to all the children in the vicinity and, in particular, to my dear friend, who had a new born baby in the house. She came and found me very distressed and said, "You will do no such thing. I and my baby will move out and you will take over my house. Your Nanny and little boy can be segregated one end, whilst you and Penelope can live in the other, where you can nurse her. So this we did and I put up dividing curtains and sheets, sprayed constantly with disinfectant, between Nanny and Francis at one end of the bungalow, and I and Penelope were segregated in the other for six weeks.

She was very seriously ill. I had to paint her throat with gentian regularly during twenty four hours each day and nurse her through the ordeal. She was only thirteen.

Our Army passages arrived and had to be cancelled. Of course, she had to be left in complete sterilized isolation. Throat swab after throat swab was always positive and the anguish of feeling that had I not kept her out in India this would not have happened was hard indeed. She was mad on swimming and I'd let her swim in Dehra Dun in the pool made for the Summer H.Q. of the Mounted Viceroy's Bodyguard, in the halcyon days when they and their Officers moved up to cooler quarters from the great heat of the Delhi plains below. From this swimming pool, which was not used in the war, she must have picked up the dyptheria germ, which seemed to be killing her. She lost three stone in weight and there were times when I thought she might die as there was no Hospital or specialist to turn to.

At this time the war in Europe had been won, and all troopships were crowded, so that if an allotted passage was not taken up, we went back to the bottom of the roster. Miraculously, after six weeks, she got one clear throat swab and her temperature dropped. Shortly after, at the hottest time of the year in June, I got offered four berths in the troopship "Monarch of Bermuda" to sail from Bombay, so I cabled acceptance. When our tough doctor heard of this, he told me that if I took my child across India in her condition in the hot weather and she died en route, I alone would be responsible for her death. I knew that if between acceptance, and the date of sailing, her temperature rose, I would not go, but I prayed, and continued to nurse her. We received our sailing date and so when it arrived, despite all, I decided to set off. She was very weak and thin and we had an appalling train journey of forty-eight hours ahead of us across the plains of India at the hottest time of the year in mid-June and then a three weeks voyage on a troopship in the monsoon.

Reggie arranged to get to Delhi on duty to meet us and we all stayed with a Brigadier cousin there for two nights in a violent dust storm, I remember, heralding the approaching monsoon, after which we continued our train journey to Bombay on the "Frontier Mail" to embark in all the chaos and heat of those docks.

My two loyal Indian servants had come with us, and saying goodbye to them, which we all knew was for ever, left us speechless. All I could do was hold their hands and the tears ran down all our faces, as I tried to say "Thank you" for everything they had done for me in those long war years.

I was lucky to have a cabin with my children and Nanny on our own, because, possibly, my husband was by then a Brigadier. The ship was crowded to capacity with troops and families going "Home" at last and as we edged out of Bombay Docks and Harbour and I left my beloved behind, I so wanted not to have to go. We had no idea when we would meet again. The Japanese war was still on, so life-belts and "black outs" were once again the order of the day. The heat in the Indian Ocean was stupendous before the break of the monsoon with all cabin windows sealed and full black-out operating. Jap. submarines were still in the Indian Ocean.

Poor old Nanny was immediately laid low with seasickness, Penelope was dreadfully frail with legs like sticks, and Francis was only five, so that there were four life jackets for me to carry about for boat drill, and not much time to sentimentalize about my last sight of the "Gateway of India".

Luckily, too, I found several friends and their children also on board, in the "same boat" literally, as myself; most without their husbands, except for a lucky few whose husbands had been repatriated.

A troopship is difficult to imagine in time of war unless one has experienced it. With little space to walk or sit, the atmosphere for most was one of thankfulness and elation that at very long last, after four to six years, to be going "Home".

At Port Said, joy of joys, the lights came on and as we ploughed through the beautiful cool breezes of the Mediterranean, and the blue European skies seemed to smile down on us, our hearts lifted at the thought of dear England so very near again.

The sea air had done wonders for Penelope, and even Nanny stopped being seasick!

As the White Cliffs really did rise dimly on the horizon, my joy was saddened by the brash ship tanoy blaring forth the news that the great Englishman, who won the war for us, Winston Churchill, had been thrown out of his high office, after all the years of "Blood, sweat, toil and tears" which he had brought us through, to Victory.

We docked at Liverpool on a perfect summer day, at 5 a.m. No porters, first surprise! So we humped our luggage on to our troop train and were deposited at a siding on the outskirts of London. From here we got into a fleet of buses to drive through the moving and terrible sight of the London we knew, so devastated by bombing. We were all very quiet then. So on to Kent, so rightly called "The Garden of England", an experience I shall never forget. The evening sun on the beauty of its greenness and flowers and glorious trees, after five long years away, were like a dream. However good the memory may be, it is impossible to remember how gloriously beautiful is the English countryside in high summer, unsurpassed anywhere else in the world. I was Home again, with all my children safe and sound. No husband still, but I felt by now at last, he was out of danger.

In fact, he had to stay in the East for another year helping to repatriate the sick, wounded, and prisoners of war of the 14th Army from Singapore. But, on a never to be forgotten day, in April, 1946, I scrambled over officials and luggage and all in sight, at Victoria Station, to throw myself into the arms of my sunburnt, laughing soldier husband as he stepped out of his troop-train from Southampton bringing him back, at last, six years after I'd gone out on a troopship to be with him.

THE END

Glossary

Annas   16 Annas = 1 Rupee

Cholera Belt   A belt worn while sleeping under a mosquito net to prevent cholera

Flit Gun   A pump action spray gun filled with insecticide.

Gay   The proper definition as used in the 1920's: light-hearted, sportive, mirthful, showy, brilliant. (Nothing to do with homosexuality).

Grass Widow   An Army wife separated from her husband by war or exercises.

I.C.S   Indian Civil Service. They administered India.

I.M.S   Indian Medical Service. They ran military & civilian hospitals in India.

Jodphurs   Trousers worn for horse riding. Named after trousers in Jodhpur.

Maharajah   An Indian Prince who ruled the Maharajah States in British India.

Memsahib   A married white or upper class woman. Mem; a variation of ma'am.

Pugarees   Indian word for turban. Also a band round a hat shielding the sun.

Rupees   The currency of India. 1 Rupee = 1s 6d   13 Rupees = 1 pound.

Sam Browne   A leather belt with supporting strap passing over the right shoulder.

Topee   A hat or cap. Like a pith helmet. From Hindi 'Topi'.